FOR THE

LOVE

OF DISCIPLINE

FOR THE
LOVE
OF DISCIPLINE

When the **Gospel** Meets
Tantrums and Time-Outs

Sara Wallace

P U B L I S H I N G
P.O. BOX 817 • PHILLIPSBURG • NEW JERSEY 08865-0817

Portions of this book have been taken from the author's writings on her blog, www.gospelcenteredmom.com, and revised and adapted for this format.

Printed in the United States of America

Library of Congress Cataloging-in-Publication Data

Names: Wallace, Sara, 1983- author.
Title: For the love of discipline : when the gospel meets tantrums and time-outs / Sara Wallace.
Description: Phillipsburg, NJ : P&R, [2018] | Includes bibliographical references.
Identifiers: LCCN 2017049695| ISBN 9781629953571 (pbk) | ISBN 9781629953588 (epub) | ISBN 9781629953595 (mobi)
Subjects: LCSH: Child rearing--Religious aspects--Christianity. | Discipline of children--Religious aspects--Christianity. | Parenting--Religious aspects--Christianity.
Classification: LCC BV4529 .W256 2018 | DDC 248.8/45--dc23
LC record available at https://lccn.loc.gov/2017049695

To my mom, Janice Thompson,
whose wisdom and grace echo in my own heart every day
and inspire me to love like Jesus.

Contents

Part 1: Lasting Motivation: Discovering the Gospel in Discipline

Part 2: Practical Tools: How Does It Really Look?

Acknowledgments

Special thanks to the following people:

My trusted counselors and fellow Master's University alumni, the "Master's Mamas," for your honesty and humor.

The seasoned mothers at Zion United Reformed Church who came alongside me as a new mom and helped me to see the big picture.

The moms at Coeur D'Alene Reformed Church who regularly join me in the back of the sanctuary as we shepherd little hearts together.

My dad, whose faithfulness I will aspire to all my life, and who predicted this book years before it existed.

My husband, for daily coming to my rescue with support, wisdom, and chocolate.

From One Mom to Another:
As You Get Started . . .

Last year I was an Awana Cubby leader. I had some skin in the game (two Cubbies of my own), so I decided it was only right for me to help out. One night I sat in the back and looked over the sea of little blue preschool vests, the kids wiggling excitedly as they listened to the Bible story from their leader. The leader stopped in the middle of the story to address a couple of distracting Cubbies. "No, Cubbies. We don't spit on each other. Listen to the story and have self-control."

I smiled to myself. *Good job, teacher,* I thought. *Don't let those little troublemakers get away with it. They need to learn self-control now while they're young. They need to be thoughtful of those around them, respectful of their teacher, and—oh, shoot. Those are my kids.*

Discipline always seems easier when we are applying it to someone else's kids, doesn't it? When it comes to our own kids, we're a mess. How do we know if we're being too hard or too soft? Why does what works for kid number one not work for kid number three? We're too close to the situation. We're emotionally and physically drained and headed toward burnout.

If you like the idea of well-disciplined kids but are finding it easier said than done, you're not alone—and this book is for you. After having five boys in just seven years, I thought about writing a book called *Lord of the Flies*, but that name was already taken. Instead I bring you this—a personal, frank, embarrassingly raw account of what God has taught me about the *D* word. I didn't write this book because discipline comes naturally to me, or because my kids are models of obedience. I wrote it because my kid pushed your kid into the pool at swim lessons. I wrote it because last week I had to leave the grocery store early when my kids were wrestling in the aisles. And I wrote it because discipline seems exhausting and discouraging only when we leave out the most important ingredient: the gospel.

There's a good chance that discipline isn't your favorite topic. But, whether you're awaiting the arrival of your first baby or you've trod this path for years already, you've recognized that it's important. Nothing brings out our frustration, our doubts about our parenting, and our random fears about our kids' futures like disobedience. When the two-year-old crumples up on the ground in a fit of anger, our hearts crumple up with him. "*Not again.*"

I want to show you a new way to look at disobedience: be glad that your children are disobeying here and now, with you as their loving parent to guide and shepherd them. The world is a cruel teacher. Satan is already hunting for their weaknesses so he can trip them up and wreak havoc on their faith and their lives. You have a chance now, in this tiny window of time, to strengthen their armor—to find the holes in their breastplates and sharpen their swords, to tweak their helmets and tighten their belts. You can't do that if they never show you where they are weak.

When your kids disobey, they are telling you something.

Strain your ears to hear past the tantrums, the rebellious stomping, and the disrespectful tone. They are saying, "Mom . . . I don't know how to obey on my own. Can you help me?"

If you're looking for a formula that will turn disobedient kids into perfect little angels, you won't find it in this book. Actually, you won't find that anywhere. God doesn't give us a formula. He gives us principles. The Holy Spirit gives us wisdom in order to use those principles to point our kids to Christ. But gospel-centered discipline starts with developing a gospel-centered mind-set—which is where we begin in this book.

The first part of the book will help us take a step back in order to see the big picture. What is gospel-centered discipline, and what is it *not*? What are the factors working against us? How can we lay a solid gospel foundation for our discipline so we aren't building on shifting sand?

The second part of this book will take us into the nitty-gritty ins and outs of discipline. Theology is wonderful—but how will it help me shepherd my screaming two-year-old? We'll take an up-close-and-personal look at specific discipline strategies that aid in big-picture gospel training. These are practical tools that will help stay-at-home moms and working moms alike.

Discipline is a beautiful privilege. We don't want our children to learn the hard way. We don't want them to disobey when it will cost them so much more than a time-out. When your children disobey, think to yourself, *Thank you for showing me your heart. Now I can help you.* Don't get discouraged. Thank God for the opportunity to shape their little hearts while they're still in your care. This is our time. This is our chance to point our kids to the only thing that matters: the gospel. God has given us the task of discipline not just in order to survive our day but to lead our kids to the cross. There is so much more to discipline than strategies, checklists, and behavior management. There's Jesus.

Part 1

LASTING MOTIVATION

Discovering the Gospel in Discipline

1

The Game Plan: Let's Get Ready

We were on vacation at the coast a few years ago. We sat at a coffee shop perched on a rocky mountainside overlooking the ocean and nervously watched our toddler explore his new surroundings. A family sitting nearby had a little girl a few months older than our son. She flitted around the rocky cliffs, and her parents smiled and told us, "She is such a free spirit! We never interfere with her independence." The people sitting around us smiled. There seemed to be an unspoken respect for these freedom-loving parents.

Until the little girl bolted across the busy street.

Her parents didn't even notice she was gone until a customer at the coffee shop looked up and screamed. Thankfully, she was not hurt. Her parents, white with horror, gathered her up and quickly left the shop amid headshakes and disapproving frowns.

Undisciplined children are not children with more freedom. They are children in exceedingly more danger—not just physically but spiritually. "Foolishness is bound up in the heart of a child" (Prov. 22:15 NASB). If that verse doesn't give you the chills, read it again. Our children are utterly incapable of freeing themselves from their own foolishness. While it is not within our power to make our children Christians, God has sovereignly placed us in their lives to help drive their foolishness out. That can happen only with loving discipline.

So what is discipline? We often associate discipline solely with consequences—something we do to our kids when they disobey. If we stop there, we will miss the depth and beauty of God's plan for discipline. The Greek word for discipline is *paideia*, which means "the whole training and educating of children, which relates to the cultivation of mind and morals."[1] Yes, discipline involves training and consequences, but that "cultivation" in the definition above takes place in the rich soil of shepherding, nourishing, and cherishing our children. Just as we feed them food to care for their bodies, our discipline feeds their minds and souls. Discipline prompts them to do what's right and prevents them from doing what's wrong.

As Christian parents we recognize that this involves hard work and pain because we will be met with resistance. But our goal is always for our kids' growth and maturity in the Lord. When we look at it in this light, we see that discipline, while sometimes unpleasant, is always good. The purpose of this book is to look at the "whole training" of our children within the context of daily, practical discipline skills.

This summer my toddler got his first splinter. The skin around it instantly got red and puffy. He was in pain and helpless to get it out on his own. I had a choice. I could let it go and risk infection and further pain, or I could get the dreaded tweezers. As much as my son hated being pinched and poked by the tweezers (and as much as I hated doing it), I knew that the short-term pain was for the long-term good. The end result was that the splinter came out and my son's hand could heal. Discipline itself is often not fun, but the bigger picture motivates us to press on.

It's helpful to look at what discipline is *not*. Discipline is not:

- a list of creative punishments
- a response to being inconvenienced
- an outlet for frustration
- embarrassment insurance for when your kids are in front of your friends

Discipline is not something we do *to* our kids, but something we do *for* them. It is a lifestyle. It doesn't need its own category; it's woven all throughout family life. But it doesn't happen by accident. When you have tiny ones, it's easy to think, *Of course we will discipline for really bad stuff, but our kids don't really need it right now.* But discipline is not a "we'll cross that bridge when we get there" situation. If you have kids, you're already at the bridge. You arrived the day they were born. You need a game plan.

Harry Randall Truman died of one of the most preventable causes known to man: he wouldn't get off the volcano. He had all the information telling him that Mt. Saint Helens was going to erupt and plenty of people willing to help him leave, but he was content to wait and see what would happen. On May 18th, 1980, he found out.[2] Saying "I'll deal with discipline when the time comes" is like saying "I'll wait until the volcano erupts, and then I'll decide what to do." True, we don't know exactly what the future holds for our parenting. But there are a few basic truths we *do* know that can help us come up with a game plan.

Discipline Is Not Optional

Organic or inorganic? Cloth diapers or disposable? To vaccinate or not to vaccinate? There are so many choices you will make as a parent. When it comes to discipline, God has not given us the option of whether to do it or not. Discipline is an inseparable part of godly parenting that we cannot choose to relinquish. Ephesians 6:4 calls us to bring our children up "in the discipline and instruction of the Lord." Proverbs 13:24 says, "He who loves [his son] is diligent to discipline him."

If you're on the fence about discipline and your head is spinning from all the different perspectives and advice, don't ask yourself *if* you're going to discipline, but rather *how*. As we will explore in this book, discipline is not something to fear. It is the greatest adventure of love you will embark on with your kids.

Often discipline seems intimidating because we don't feel qualified. And, on our own, we are not qualified. But our call to discipline is not based on our own merits. It's not because we are smarter than our kids or because we are bigger than they are. As the authority in our homes, we reflect God's authority. Nothing could be more humbling. Discipline is an opportunity to reflect the character of God, not our own pride. In *Shepherding a Child's Heart*, Tedd Tripp says,

> God calls you to exercise authority, not in making your children do what you want, but in being true servants—authorities who lay down our lives. The purpose for your authority in the lives of your children is not to hold them under your power, but to empower them to be self-controlled people living freely under the authority of God.[3]

Not only does this humble us, but it should inspire us to be diligent to discipline our kids every day. We represent God, and God does not sit down on the job. If we are lax in our discipline, we know we have an enemy who is waiting for an opportunity. We must "be sober-minded; be watchful. Your adversary the devil prowls around like a roaring lion, seeking someone to devour" (1 Peter 5:8). We are engaged in a battle for our kids' hearts. We are on the front lines for the sake of our kids before they are even old enough to know the spiritual forces working against them.

Disciplined Kids Mean Disciplined Parents

When I was a teacher, I remember a colleague saying, "You can't teach what you are not." It didn't really start to sink in until I had kids. If I was going to set expectations for them, I had to make sure I was ready to model those expectations. I saw a meme floating around Facebook that captures this idea from a mom's perspective: "My child will only be as in charge of his emotions as I am of mine." Ouch.

The first step in disciplining our kids is disciplining ourselves. When we fail to set a good example, we still have a beautiful opportunity to point our kids to the love and forgiveness we have in Christ. This has a chain reaction: they look to us and we look to Christ, ultimately channeling their vision to our glorious God. If our eyes aren't fixed on Christ, our kids will look to us and find a dead end. We need to be in God's Word and on our knees on a regular basis. Our kids will say what we say, act the way we act, and begin to view God the way we view God. Do our words and actions show our kids that God is worthy to be obeyed? Do our lives reflect the peace that can be found only in Christ?

Take a look at your daily routine. If someone asked your kids what your priorities were, what do you think they would say? If you're in the "little years," you might be in survival mode. Your priority is probably just to get through the next minute. I get that. There are seasons of life when the laundry is never done and Mommy lives in her PJs. But your kids see what lies beyond the chaos. They can tell if Mommy answers to a higher authority. They can see that the family is working together toward a common goal, whether it's entertainment, money, or God's glory. Through periods of joy, grief, financial hardship, and plenty, our response to life should show our kids that God is good and he is in control. Can you reflect all of that to your kids and stay in your PJs all day? Absolutely. Relax. Your testimony to your kids doesn't revolve around how many items you check off your to-do list. It's about your attitude through the good, the bad, and the sticky spots on the floor.

Why is it important to discipline our own attitudes while we simultaneously shepherd our kids? I realized recently that I don't have the luxury of sighing and moaning under my breath when I'm hauling a load of laundry into the living room because, if I do, there is sure to be a little voice that immediately copies me. Parenting provides a whole new layer of accountability in our lives. There is always someone listening, always someone watching. Yesterday, at lunchtime, the three-year-old spilled his milk. Before I could say anything, his brother exclaimed in an exasperated voice, "Oh, for heaven's sake!" I frowned and thought, *That doesn't sound very kind and compassionate. Oh, wait. That sounds exactly like me.*

What about when we fail? If my kids modeled my behavior on certain days, I would have five little boys stomping around the house, short-tempered, discontent, and self-centered. What a disaster! The beauty of the gospel is that it is custom-made for imperfect mommies. Jesus said, "Those who are well have no need of a physician, but those who are sick" (Matt. 9:12). We are all sick. So are our kids. We all need a physician for our souls.

There is no need to pretend we have our acts together. Our kids will see us sin. They will also see what we do with our sin. I can spend valuable energy trying to cover up my failures, or I can use them to point my kids to the gospel. I can say, "Mommy was having a bad attitude. We all have bad attitudes sometimes, don't we? My attitude was sinful. That's why I'm so glad I have Jesus to forgive me! I am not perfect, but Jesus is perfect. His perfect attitude can take the place of my sinful attitude."

You and I have work to do, don't we? Thankfully, the greatest work of all has already been accomplished for us. Through Christ's work on the cross we are free to love God and be loved by him. We can trust him to work through us for his glory even when we are at our weakest. We can say with Paul, "For the sake of Christ, then, I am content with weaknesses. . . . For when I am weak, then I am strong" (2 Cor. 12:10). God doesn't work around our weakness—he works *through* it. We can confidently walk in his love in a way that reflects his holy character to our children.

Discipline Is Not a Quick Fix

Yesterday I loaded the kids into the van to run errands. Between the time I buckled them in and the time I went inside to grab my purse and keys, everything had fallen apart. They were screaming at each other, fighting, and generally making a pack of caged wolves look like puppies.

"All right, everybody out," I said. We filed back into the house, and one by one each child was held accountable for his part in the chaos. Talks were had, consequences were given, and tears were dried. We piled back into the car, all of us worse for wear. We went through our errands tired, sniffly, and disheveled. *We're a mess,* I thought as I wiped tears of frustration from my own eyes at the stoplight. *What happened? I did what I was supposed to do. I took the time; I disciplined the kids; I prioritized their hearts over my carefully planned errands. Why are we all still so miserable?*

If you have committed yourself to faithfully disciplining

your kids according to God's Word and it's a lot messier than you thought, it doesn't necessarily mean you are doing something wrong. It means that discipline is a long-term commitment. As with any commitment, we can't say, "I'll give this thing a shot, but if I don't see the results I want when I want them, I'm out." If that were our attitude, it would take about two days for all of us to throw in the towel.

Discouragement in discipline often reveals a heart set on a quick fix. If you go into discipline knowing it's a slow process, you are less likely to lose your steam. This goes against our fast-paced, results-oriented culture. Michael Horton in his book *Ordinary* says,

> The problem is not that we are too active, but that we are recklessly frenetic. We have grown accustomed to quick fixes and easy solutions. We have grown accustomed to running sprints instead of training for the long-distance marathon. We have plenty of energy. The danger is that we will burn ourselves out on restless anxieties and unrealistic expectations.[4]

Are our expectations realistic when it comes to discipline? Is our ultimate goal God's glory or our own desired outcomes?

In Hebrews 11 we read about the heroes of the faith, such as Abraham, Moses, and David. If these godly people had set their eyes on a specific earthly outcome, they would have been greatly disappointed. Hebrews 11:13 says, "These all died in faith, *not* having received the things promised, but having seen them and greeted them from afar, and having acknowledged that they were strangers and exiles on the earth." I think about that when my hard work with the kids doesn't seem to be paying off. Instead of getting discouraged, I remember I am "greeting my reward from afar." I am an alien here. I am working against culture, against sin in my kids, and against sin in my own heart. If my discipline seems strange on this planet, it's because it is accomplishing heavenly goals.

I don't know how God will use my discipline. I am hopeful that I will see much fruit from it this side of heaven, but frankly that's none of my business. I'm just the bricklayer. Every time I lovingly and intentionally discipline my kids for God's glory, I lay another brick. I don't know exactly what God is building in my kids. Will my toddler start staying in bed after just two days, or will this go on for months? Will my six-year-old be cured of his back talk through my discipline, or will he have a lifelong battle with respect for authority? I don't know. But I don't need to know in order to obey God's plan for discipline.

That doesn't mean discipline is a shot in the dark. Scripture gives us much guidance and much hope. Proverbs 22:6 says, "Train up a child in the way he should go; even when he is old he will not depart from it." While not a surefire promise that our kids will be Christians, this verse is a beautiful encouragement that the truth we teach our kids now will stick with them forever—however God chooses to use it. Scripture tells us that "a wise son makes a glad father" (Prov. 15:20) and that a faithful mother's children will "rise up and call her blessed" (Prov. 31:28). We know that godly mothers are often the means that God uses to raise up faithful leaders in the church, such as Timothy: "I am reminded of your sincere faith, a faith that dwelt first in your grandmother Lois and your mother Eunice and now, I am sure, dwells in you as well" (2 Tim. 1:5).

Elyse Fitzpatrick, in her book *Give Them Grace*, helps us strike that balance of working and hoping:

> We work because we love him and all he's done for us. We work because he's commanded us to work. And we work because

he may use our efforts at parenting as the means to draw our children to him. But we are never to work because we think our work will ultimately transform our children. Our works are never good enough or powerful enough to transform any human heart.[5]

God can use our discipline however he wants. Our job is to faithfully lay those bricks—even though it sometimes seems to take the mortar a *long* time to set. Your discipline might be messy, but it is never fruitless. God will always glorify himself through our obedience.

Reflection

1. What does the word *discipline* make you think of? Does this word have positive or negative connotations for you, and why?
2. Proverbs 3:12 says, "For the LORD reproves him whom he loves, as a father the son in whom he delights." How does this verse further explain why discipline is not optional?
3. In what specific ways do you want to be a more disciplined parent? Reflect on habits you want to change or begin.
4. What comfort can you fall back on when discipline doesn't seem to be working quickly enough? Write a short prayer or a Scripture passage from the chapter to meditate on this week.

2

Why We Don't "Punish" Our Kids

As you know, this is a book about discipline. There is a word usually connected with this topic that will be noticeably absent from this book. In secular culture (and often in the church as well), *discipline* is used synonymously with the word *punishment*—but punishment and discipline are fundamentally different. "You're splitting hairs," some might say. "Stop with the word games and tell me how long to put my toddler in time-out!" I'm right there with you. But trust me—these are hairs worth splitting. We're laying the foundation for that long-term, messy commitment we talked about. We're shepherding hearts, not just fixing bad behavior. So let's start with some glorious heart stuff.

In 2013, sixteen-year-old Cooper Van Huizen was sentenced to one to fifteen years in prison for stealing his father's gun. The gun was used in a violent burglary, and the boy was held responsible for providing it. His family sobbed as he was led away to a maximum-security prison. Cold, hard justice had been served.[1]

Switch scenes. Now the setting is my living room. The four-year-old just wrecked his brother's Lego pirate ship (with a mischievous grin, of course). Court is in session. A brief defense is given by both parties. A decision is made, and a consequence is given. But this is where a Christian home takes a dramatic shift away from a courtroom. The boy in the court case above was punished. My son will face something very different: discipline.

The word *punishment* shares the root "pun" with words like *punitive* and *penalty*. *Punitive, penalty,* and *punishment* all have to do with a set of laws and what happens when they are broken. Punishment is retributive. It means getting exactly what is deserved for an offense committed. As incredible as it sounds, that will never happen to God's people. Punishment is no longer part of our relationship with God. Every drop of punishment was absorbed for us by Christ on the cross. God is not our judge anymore. He is our Father. We will never, never be punished for our sins. Instead, as part of our new punishment-free relationship with him, we will be lovingly disciplined. Pastor and author Paul Tautges says, "God as Father never looks at us as guilty, only as beloved children who are being foolish or wayward or even rebellious and insolent. Our sin grieves him, but it does not provoke vengeance."[2]

Discipline may look and feel similar to punishment, but they are radically different. Discipline has a completely different motivation: love. Discipline doesn't seek retribution. It genuinely seeks the best for the other person. Punishment looks to the law. Discipline looks to grace. A good word to work into our vocabulary in place of *punishment* is *consequences*. Instead of saying, "I'm going to punish you," we can say, "Your sin has consequences." One sounds like payback and the other sounds like a natural outcome. One is a dead end and the other is productive. Consequences show our kids that sin goes against God's plan. When we choose our own way instead of God's way, bad things happen.

The consequences that we give our kids now prepare them to avoid much greater consequences later in life. That's why consequences and grace go hand in hand. For us as Christians, God will only allow consequences that work for our good and his glory. Grace might still involve pain for God's people, but it is a purposeful pain. The goal of discipline (whether it feels pleasant or not) is to conform us to the image of Christ. What could be better for us than that?

So how does this relate to parenting? We want to be parents who discipline rather than punish. Discipline is actually part of our love language to our kids. Rather than fearing our loving discipline, our kids will thrive under it. First John reminds us that "there is no fear in love, but perfect love casts out fear. For fear has to do with punishment, and whoever fears has not been perfected in love" (1 John 4:18). Verse 17 tells us that fear is tied to judgment. Since we have been set free from the fear of punishment and judgment, we want to mimic the merciful discipline we receive from our heavenly father. While we don't necessarily know whether our children are Christians, this is one of the most tangible ways we can point them to the hope of a Savior. Let's take a closer look at how discipline is different from punishment on a practical level.

Discipline Seeks a Changed Heart

When the judge sentenced the sixteen-year-old boy, he checked him off the list and moved on to the next case. There was no follow-up between the judge and the boy. Why would there be? Justice had been served, and that's all that punishment requires. Isn't it easy sometimes for us to punish our kids in order to check off a parental duty? We have to catch ourselves to see if we are taking time to address the heart. While punishment says, "I'm only concerned with what you did," discipline says, "I'm also concerned with *why* you did that."

When my four-year-old wrecked the pirate ship, punitive justice would have given a very logical consequence: he must rebuild it and won't get to play with anything else until he does. While loving discipline might give the same consequence, creating a teachable moment as well takes more time. In this instance I asked my son, "Was what you did kind? We want to be kind to each other, because Jesus is so kind to us. How can you show kindness to your brother?" When we talk to our kids, we're careful to use words like *consequence* and *discipline* rather than *punishment*.

I have to be honest—this is the most exhausting part of parenting for me. There are so many times it would be easier to revert to being a cold, objective judge. I could dole out the consequences and go back to making dinner. But I have to remind myself that I am constantly painting an image of God for my children. Tedd Tripp reminds us that "you must direct your children on God's behalf for their good."[3] I represent God to my kids. Do they see God as a judge or as a shepherd? When I take time to discipline their hearts, I pave the way for gospel hope.

Discipline Seeks a Changed Relationship

Think how odd it would have been if the judge in the courtroom had jumped up from his seat and thrown his arms around the boy. It would have been strange because punishment doesn't require any kind of relationship between the judge and the guilty party. We want *relationship* with our children—not just for our sakes, but to point them to the relationship that is possible with Jesus Christ. True relationship with our kids is impossible without discipline. Discipline actually *proves* sonship.

The writer of Hebrews makes this unmistakable connection for us:

It is for discipline that you have to endure. God is treating you as sons. For what son is there whom his father does not discipline? If you are left without discipline, in which all have participated, then you are illegitimate children and not sons. (Heb. 12:7–8)

A.W. Pink says, "Chastisement evidences our Divine sonship: the father of a family does not concern himself with those on the outside: but those within he guides and disciplines to make them conform to his will. . . . Look beyond the rod to the All-wise hand that wields it!"[4] I love that word *concern*. A father's discipline expresses concern over the well-being of his child.

Pastor Doug Thompson of Middletown Bible Church in California expresses it this way: "There is only one thing worse for a kid than being spanked, or grounded, or having the cell phone or computer . . . taken away . . . : being neglected."[5]

We often function as though we have two options when our kids disobey: to punish or to ignore. Discipline does neither. It peels back the layers of sinful actions in order to deal with underlying causes and attitudes. Punishment looks to the past at what has already been done. Discipline looks to the hope of the future. It is proactive, saying, "I don't care about what you did as much as I care about what it means for your future if we don't deal with it now."

Punishment is easier than discipline. We are wired for justice. Our short tempers fuel our inner judge. Discipline requires patience, wisdom, and love. The next time an offense is committed in your home, remember how your Father treats you when you sin. Address it head on, but seek the heart. Seek relationship. Remember that you've been entrusted with the caregiving staff of a shepherd, not the gavel of a judge.

Reflection

1. Explain why punishment is not part of a Christian's relationship with God but discipline is.
2. Why is punishment sometimes easier than discipline?
3. How does discipline point our kids to the gospel? Refer back to Hebrews 12:7–8.
4. In what specific ways can you parent less like a justice-centered judge and more like a heart-centered shepherd? (Example: When the kids aren't sharing, a judge might say, "Who had it first?" A shepherd might say, "How can you prefer the other person in love?")

3

Rewards and the Gospel

As we consider discipline in light of relationship, it causes us to see it in a much more positive light. It helps us to see that discipline isn't just about how we handle bad behavior but also about how we address good behavior. What do we do when our kids obey? How do we draw attention to it so our kids can learn from their successes and not just their failures?

If we're going to imitate our heavenly Father in our discipline, we can't leave out his generous, lavish goodness. James 1:17 says, "Every good gift and every perfect gift is from above, coming down from the Father of lights." Psalm 84:11 says, "The LORD bestows favor and honor. No good thing does he withhold from those who walk uprightly." We want to shower our kids with the blessings that come from walking in God's ways.

A very practical way to do this is through rewards. Rewards can be an effective, tangible way to point our kids to the gospel. But, just as with our consequences, we have to be strategic, intentional, and balanced when it comes to rewarding our kids.

When I was a third grade teacher, I had a student who was constantly behind on his work. He was very smart, but he naturally moved very slowly. I made a special little chart for him so that he would earn a sticker every time he finished an assignment within the time limit I set. When he filled up his chart, he got a prize from the prize box. It seemed to help, but once he earned his prize he would start to slow down again, and we would have to start the chart over.

At the end of the school year the students had to write a letter of advice to the class coming up. The topic of the letter was "How to Survive Mrs. Wallace's Class." When I read the note from my slow student, I had to smile and roll my eyes. He wrote, "In the beginning of the year, do all of your schoolwork as slowly as you can. Then Mrs. Wallace will give you a sticker chart, and when you do your work quickly you will get a prize."

This reward accomplished the short-term goal of teaching him a new skill, but that was only the beginning. Rewards are not an end in themselves. They are a means to a much greater end. Ultimately, I didn't want my student to conform to my standards just for a prize. I wanted him to appreciate the benefits of a faithful work ethic.

We can use rewards as a stepping-stone toward the greater goal of addressing the heart. But this can be tricky. How can we use rewards to address the heart and not just outward behavior? And, more importantly, how can we use rewards to point our children to the gospel?

John Piper says, "Children are born legalists. . . . They believe that the only path to morality is keeping the law—parents' law, school law, baby sitter's law, traffic law, whatever, law, law, law. Everywhere is law, because these kids are just being told what to do all the time from the time they are nine months old on up." That law is not bad. God created us to think this way in order to point us to the gospel. Piper goes on to say, "The alternative to this thinking is the gospel of the glory of Christ—seeing parents who love Christ so much that Christ looks appealing to them, not mainly as a law giver, but a soul satisfier, a friend, a guide, a helper, a counselor and, yes, a final, absolute authority."[1]

So the big question is, how can we use rewards to make Christ more appealing to our kids without feeding their natural legalistic tendencies? We don't want the rewards to stop at the dead end of good works. But there is a way to use them as a springboard to the gospel. It all comes down to the *focus* of the reward. I've found three questions that help me determine this focus.

God or Self?

Does the reward point our kids to God or to themselves? Scripture gives us a clear connection between obedience and reward (or blessing). Ephesians 6:2–3 says that children who obey their parents will "live long in the land." In Deuteronomy 6:3, God tells his people that if we obey, it will "go well with" us.

Here is where we need to make an important distinction: the point of these passages is not to point us back to our own good works but rather to point us to the character of God. Obedience to God yields blessing because of *his* good character, not ours. We receive blessing when we obey because God is good. The blessings of obedience point us back to a God who is worthy to be obeyed. How does this look practically? Take a look at these examples of how to direct kids' hearts to God instead of to themselves:

- We obey Mom and Dad because that's how we obey God. When you say yes to Mom, you say yes to God!
- We forgive our brothers and sisters because God forgives us—even though we don't deserve it.

35

- We don't fuss because God has given us so much to be thankful for. What are some things you can thank God for today?
- We share our toys because God is so generous with us.
- We have self-control in the grocery store because that is kind to other people. When other people see us being kind, they see an example of Jesus.

One of my favorite devotional books to read with my kids is Susan Hunt's *My ABC Bible Verses: Hiding God's Word in Little Hearts*. In every chapter, the children in the stories are reminded that the strength to obey comes from God. In one chapter, the dad says, "The Holy Spirit shines the light of God's truth into our hearts. Then, when we obey God's Word, we shine that light out so others can see it. When you give a soft answer, or when you are a peacemaker, or when you keep your tongue from evil, the light of God's truth shines through you."[2]

What a wonderful way to keep the focus of our obedience on God. Robert Murray M'Cheyne said, "For every look at yourself, take ten looks at Christ."[3] Everything we do in our parenting should tell our kids, "Look to Jesus." As we reward our children for growing in good deeds, we want them to see that God gets all the glory. Instead of the reward saying, "Yay; look what you did!" it says, "Yay; look what God is doing in your heart!" Our kids begin to see that the greatest reward of all is participating in bringing glory to God.

Action or the Heart?

Does the reward address *only* the outward actions, or does it aim for the heart? A good friend of mine made a reward chart for her son about the fruit of the Spirit. She listed out the fruit (love, joy, peace, patience, kindness, goodness, faithfulness, gentleness, and self-control), and her son got a sticker each time she caught him practicing a fruit of the Spirit.

Now, this could have gone two different ways. If the chart focused just on outward actions, it would have fed her son's natural legalistic tendencies and taught him to pat himself on the back. It would have fostered self-reliance and taught him how to comply on the outside in order to get what he wanted. But my friend went for the heart. She didn't just want to change her son's behavior. She laid important groundwork first.

"None of us can show all of the fruit of the Spirit perfectly," she told him. "But do you know who did? Jesus showed *all* of the fruit of the Spirit *all* the time! He did it for us. With the help of the Holy Spirit we can show this beautiful fruit, too. We love this fruit because Jesus loves this fruit. When we show this fruit, we look like Jesus!"

It's natural for kids to obey only for the reward at first. That's how we get their attention. My friend's son had to show the appropriate action in order to get the sticker. But each time her son got a sticker for showing one of the fruits, she pointed him back to Jesus. He learned to associate the rewards with the beauty of the Savior instead of just his own accomplishments.

Heavenly Perspective or Earthly Perspective?

Finally, does the reward develop a heavenly perspective within our children? More and more I am aware of the fact that this world is not our home. I want to raise my children to know that too. Not every good deed receives an earthly reward. The blessings that God promises his people are often heavenly. We might not see the rewards of our obedience in this lifetime. Instead, we might experience the opposite. First Peter 3:17

talks about suffering for doing good. First Peter 2:23 says that Jesus experienced persecution for his obedience. Instead of insisting on his reward from God, he "continued entrusting himself to him who judges justly." Jesus knew his reward was a heavenly one.

Our children are too young to fully grasp heavenly rewards, because they can't see them. The rewards we give them, whether they be a sticker or a toy or a candy, help to paint a picture of a heavenly reality. But we have to be careful. If my kids hold out their hands for a reward every time they obey, I know their perspective has gotten off balance. I want them to associate the rewards I give them with a far greater reward that is to come.

In our backyard, the kids have a favorite swing. It is often the source of much fighting and tension. A couple of days ago, the five-year-old was swinging and his brother came marching toward him. Without thinking twice, the five-year-old hopped off the swing and said, "You can have a turn!" I was just about knocked off my feet. I was tempted to do something for him—to give him a reward or something else fun that he could do. But the look on his face was so happy. He was soaking up the reward of pleasing God. And that was enough.

It was a good reminder for me that the rewards I give my kids are only a placeholder for an appreciation of eternal, spiritual rewards. As they start to develop that on their own, the rewards that I give them have served their purpose. Even when there are no earthly rewards around, I want them to feel that sense of reward on the inside.

We can start fostering that eternal perspective now. It starts with telling our kids *why* we obey. It's not to get candy or a sticker or a toy. It's because a great eternal reward has been purchased for those who believe in Christ. Our ultimate reward will be sharing in Christ's glory when he comes again—when God says, "Well done, good and faithful servant. . . . Enter into the joy of your master" (Matt. 25:23).

A Word on Bribes

There is a fine line between rewarding and bribing. A bribe doesn't take that final, important step of pointing the child to Christ. It ends at the behavior. The child sees no other reason to do what the parent is asking other than receiving the promised treat. Kids can even decide for themselves whether the bribe is worth it or not. A bribe says, "If you get off the swing and come to the car right now, I will give you a cookie." The child swings her legs, thinks about it, and decides, "Nah. I've had enough cookies today. I think I'll keep swinging." The parent might then try to make the treat more appealing. "All right, two cookies." There is no appeal to the heart. Bribery communicates only with our fleshly desires. Cookie or swing? Which one sounds better at the time?

We've seen that rewards highlight and celebrate obedience, but the main focus of a bribe is disobedience. Either the child is already disobeying and the parent is trying to make him stop, or else the parent assumes that without the bribe the child will disobey. It usually sounds something like "If you stop screaming, I will give you candy." Instead of giving the child much needed discipline, a bribe seeks to make a trade. The parent essentially says, "If you give me what I want, I'll give you what you want."

This distorts the beautiful picture of how God rewards his people. He rewards us in his lavish mercy and grace, as a way to point us to his love. It's a beautiful, mutual celebration: we celebrate God, and he celebrates us.

A treat should never take the place of discipline. When we give our kids an incentive to obey, we need to ask ourselves, "Am l celebrating his obedience or simply doing damage control for disobedience?" A reward is appropriate for one, whereas discipline is more appropriate for the other.

A bribe might seem like a quick fix, but the results are short-lived. Rewards that address the heart take more time and intentionality, but the end results are authentic and lasting.

Reflection

1. Think of a skill or character trait you want your child to work on. How might you use rewards to help your child grow in this area while still pointing him or her to the gospel?
2. What is the danger in rewarding without giving careful thought to how we talk about the rewards?
3. Read Psalm 19:11 (which refers to God's commandments) and Philippians 2:13. Who gets the credit for our obedience?
4. How could you use 1 Corinthians 10:31 to explain to your child why we obey?

4

The Right Kind of Fear

Why bring up the subject of fear in a book about discipline? Rightly placed fear fuels productive, gospel-centered discipline, while misplaced fear works against us. As we have already seen, the world's philosophy of discipline revolves around fear of punishment. For Christian parents, discipline revolves around fear, too—but it's not fear of punishment. It is fear of God. Psalm 111:10 says, "The fear of the LORD is the beginning of wisdom." If this is where wisdom starts, then this is where our discipline should start. When we regularly and intentionally teach our kids to fear God, our discipline says, "There is a God who is worthy to be obeyed. Look at how beautiful and holy he is. We love him, and we love his holiness."

Last week, I leaned over to kiss my five-year-old good night when I heard whimpering in the bed across the room. My six-year-old, who had just hopped happily into bed moments before, was huddled under his blankets. "What's wrong?" I asked as I walked over to his bed and sat on the edge.

"I had a bad dream last night, and I'm afraid I'll have it again."

I stroked his head. "I've had bad dreams before, too. Try to remember that they're not real."

"But what if I can't do that?" he moaned. "What if I forget or I'm not strong enough?"

His words tugged at my heart. I knew exactly how he felt. My son is a deep thinker. His own faithlessness was scarier to him than the monsters in the dark. His words echoed the feelings of my own heart at many points in my life.

I smiled and said, "You don't have to think about what *you* can do. Think about what *God* can do. You will never be strong enough to face scary things on your own, but God is always strong enough. He never changes." My son's face burst into a smile. It clicked. I was thrilled, because I often get that glazed-over look that says, "Thanks, Mom, but . . . can I just have a bigger night-light?"

As I walked out of his room he said, "I'm going to think about that, Mom. I'm going to think about all the things God can do."

I said, "I'm so glad. I'm going to think about it too."

Telling my son, "Your bad dreams aren't real," was an attempt to eliminate his fear. It didn't work very well. Telling him, "God is stronger than your bad dreams, and he's stronger than you," *replaced* his fears. Without realizing it, he switched the object of his fear to something else—something real and infinitely greater. By attributing to God strength that was bigger than his bad dreams, he was *fearing* God. Fearing his dreams gave him misery. Fearing God gave him hope.

In C. S. Lewis's book *The Lion, the Witch, and the Wardrobe*, Mr. Beaver gives a perfect summary of what it looks like to fear God. Susan asks him whether Aslan the lion is safe, to which he responds, "Who said anything about safe? 'Course he isn't safe. But he's good."[1] Fear of God produces comfort. We love him not because he is safe but because he is *not* safe—and yet we are completely protected in him. The God who should have been our destroyer is now our Savior. We are saved from God himself *by* God himself. Once again the gospel turns human logic on its head and creates an entirely new reality. Through forgiveness in Jesus Christ we now experience a fear we can hide *in* rather than hide *from*. I love the picture of Isaiah the prophet coming into the actual presence of God. Watch how his utter horror changes into elation and joy:

> And I said: "Woe is me! For I am lost; for I am a man of unclean lips, and I dwell in the midst of a people of unclean lips; for my eyes have seen the King, the LORD of hosts!"
>
> Then one of the seraphim flew to me, having in his hand a burning coal that he had taken with tongs from the altar. And he touched my mouth and said: "Behold, this has touched your lips; your guilt is taken away, and your sin atoned for."
>
> And I heard the voice of the Lord saying, "Whom shall I send, and who will go for us?" Then I said, "Here I am! Send me." (Isa. 6:5–8)

Isaiah thought he was dead when he saw the Lord—and he should have been. But the moment his sin was seared away by the burning coal, his agony turned to joy. "Pick me! Pick me!" were his very next words to the Lord. Instead of running from the presence of God, he jumped up and down with his hand in the air, begging to be used by the Lord. Let's take a look at the beautiful fruit that this kind of fear produces in our kids.

They Will Learn to Trust God instead of Themselves

Isaiah's confidence had nothing to do with how much better he felt about himself. It was all about who loved and accepted him. When we tell our kids "Don't be afraid," and we stop short of pointing them to our almighty God, we inadvertently point them to strength in man and in themselves. The world's mantra is "You can do it. Believe in yourself." That's a cheap comfort and a frail assurance. We have the incredible privilege of telling our kids, "God can do it. Believe in him."

Real confidence comes from outside ourselves. If I teach my son to be brave because he is strong, what will happen on days when he feels weak? When he is an adult, what will happen to his confidence when he loses his job or wrecks his car? If all of his assurances growing up were based on his own strength, his failures would be the end of his hope. I want to show my kids that our hope stretches beyond the limitations of our own strength. "Don't be afraid of what might happen. Don't be afraid of failing. God is strong enough."

There is danger in neglecting to teach our kids to fear God. If God is not to be feared, he is not to be trusted. I had a friend growing up who knew about God but did not fear him. Whenever he hit failure, he had to reinvent himself. By the time he was an adult he had already experimented with half a dozen religions, drugs, and identities. He was aware of God's presence, but in his eyes God was weak and unreliable. It was up to him to decide his own destiny. We don't want our kids to trust in themselves. We want to guide their feet to the rock that is God's character, not to the shifting sands of their own abilities.

Fear of God Points to the Gospel

The gospel creates a strange environment in which total humility and total confidence can exist in harmony. There is no other religious system in the world that does that. Tim Keller says, "There's a huge boldness to know that he loves me and also a deep humility knowing that I'm a sinner saved only by grace. And those two things grow together in a Christian, whereas I don't think they grow apart from a knowledge of the cross."² Fear makes us aware of our need for forgiveness, and forgiveness actually produces more fear. It's a beautiful cycle that drives us deeper and deeper into the gospel. We fear the One we offended, who could have destroyed us yet chose to forgive us. If God is not to be feared, there is no need for salvation. What would we need to be saved from?

We have a legacy to pass on to our children. I'm not talking about Grandma's meat loaf recipe or that embarrassing middle name that has stuck around for generations. Our legacy is the fear of the Lord. Our commitment comes straight from Psalm 78:4–7.

> We will not hide them from their children,
>   but tell to the coming generation
> the glorious deeds of the LORD, and his might,
>   and the wonders that he has done.
>
> He established a testimony in Jacob
>   and appointed a law in Israel,
> which he commanded our fathers
>   to teach to their children,
> that the next generation might know them,
>   the children yet unborn,
> and arise and tell them to their children,
>   so that they should set their hope in God
> and not forget the works of God,
>   but keep his commandments.

Fear of God Impacts Our Discipline

The fear of God is the backdrop of gospel-centered discipline. It helps both parent and child keep their roles in the proper perspective. Discipline is all about God and not about us. When we forget to teach our kids to fear God, our discipline becomes man-centered. It says, "You should obey me because I am in charge. I am bigger, stronger, and smarter than you." As daily disciplinarians, we get hung up on our authority. When we regularly point our kids to an awesome God, our discipline will naturally point them to his authority. The buck doesn't stop with Mom and Dad. We are all accountable to someone so much greater. Our discipline channels the very love and authority of God, not our own pride and desire for power. It might seem like a subtle difference, but it is not lost on our kids. They can see it.

How Do We Teach Our Kids the Fear of God?

When I was growing up, I always associated the biblical meaning of fear with respect. Respect is an appropriate synonym, but I've recently been struck by another great substitute: awe. Respect can be done purely out of duty. We can pay the right lip service to the things in life that we know we should respect. Awe is different. Awe is an emotional reaction. In one of my favorite articles by Jen Wilkin, she reminds us that awe helps us to "understand both our insignificance within creation and our significance to our Creator." She goes on to write, "You can tell me that I am a royal daughter of the King. . . . But I beg you: *Don't tell me who I am until you have caused me to gaze in awe at 'I Am.'*" Wilkin adds that statements like this contain precious truths, but their "preciousness cannot be properly perceived until framed in the brilliance of his utter holiness."[3] Let's teach our kids respect in the context of awe.

Teach Awe in Times of Fear

How can we teach our kids to stand in awe of God? A practical way comes down to how we handle their fears in the little years. Take a look at the examples below. The "Man-centered awe" examples on the left are not bad answers to our kids' fears, but they are insufficient on their own. We need to be intentional about how we create "God-centered awe" when we answer our kids' concerns.

Man-Centered Awe	God-Centered Awe
You don't have to be afraid of the dark because the bathroom light is on and Mom and Dad are right around the corner.	You don't have to be afraid of the dark because God can see in the dark and he can see you. He made the darkness, and nothing scary can hide from God.
You don't have to be afraid of germs because scientists have discovered some great ways to fight diseases.	You don't have to be afraid of germs because God made the world and he is in control of all things—even things that are too tiny to see, like germs.
You don't have to be afraid of Mom and Dad dying because we are very healthy and very careful.	You don't have to be afraid of Mom and Dad dying because God is in charge of the future. We can trust his plan, no matter what.

You can see how it would be perfectly appropriate to use both answers to comfort our kids. But, while the world stops at the first box, we have the amazing privilege of offering our kids an even deeper comfort.

Teach Awe in Times of Blessing

Last week there was a double rainbow stretched across the sky. The kids had just gone to bed, but I ran and got them all up and took them outside to see it. We were amazed. We stood there for a long time counting the rings and talking about the colors. We talked about how the light bounced off the tiny little raindrops. We were about to go inside when it hit me that we had left out the most important part of the rainbow: its Creator! We took some time to praise God right out loud. "Thank you for the beautiful rainbow, God! You are amazing!" It was a reminder to me that I have to be intentional about teaching my kids the fear of God. In her article "Utter Dark Sayings to Your Children," Rachel Watson reminds us of the importance that God places on not letting our kids forget him:

> We need to talk with them about what God has accomplished in our lives, in the lives of our friends, in human history, in his Word. Stories of his faithfulness should flood our living rooms and be stacked high on our night tables. Stories of his creation, his hard-to-fathom knowledge, and his extravagant love in Christ should be so often on our lips that the idea of forgetting him causes us to gasp.[4]

Let's show our kids how amazing God is in every part of his creation, power, and control. When a meal tastes good, say, "Isn't God amazing that he made such yummy food?" When you get home from a trip, say, "God is so good and powerful to keep us safe." Don't miss a chance to give God the credit he deserves. Take advantage of every opportunity you can to point your kids to the fear that vanquishes all other fears—the fear that gives life.

Reflection

1. Read Proverbs 9:10. Why is properly placed fear crucial to our discipline?
2. How is fear of God directly related to love for God?
3. Teaching our kids to fear God makes our discipline less about us and more about their relationship to God. How might this affect our temptation to discipline in anger?
4. How does teaching our kids to fear God put our own authority in perspective, both for us and for them?

5

Too Much or Too Little?

Do you consider yourself to be strict or lenient? I recently polled a group of friends with this question. Out of eighteen moms, the results were split straight down the middle. "Oh, I'm definitely strict," said one. "I expect my kids to obey." Another mom said, "I'm more lenient. I don't make a bunch of rules just to try to control my kids." What stood out to me the most was how negatively each mom viewed the other side. *Lenient* meant not expecting obedience. *Strict* meant meanness and unnecessary rules. It revealed to me just how subjective these words are. The reality is that we are all somewhere in between. But we need to understand the two extremes of discipline in order to see how the gospel helps us hit that sweet balance.

I remember visiting a new church with my husband when we were young parents. It was filled with other young families. As we attended a few Bible studies and potlucks, we started noticing a very subtle division in the church—an almost imperceptible line in the sand. It wasn't about the style of worship music, church attire, or kids' programs. It was about discipline.

As I talked with a few of the moms, I realized this division had created cliques within the church. It came down to two groups. The first group thought that the second group disciplined too much. The second group thought that the first group disciplined too little. While trying to enjoy church gatherings and playdates, every mom could feel the tension. There were hurt feelings and insecurities. Everyone felt they had to choose a side. One mom told me, "I don't know where I fit in here."

The tension this church was experiencing is the same tension I feel in my own heart every day. Am I disciplining too much or too little? Most times, I walk away from a discipline situation thinking I was either too harsh or too lenient. True biblical discipline, motivated by love and the example of our heavenly Father, helps us strike a balance we could never strike on our own.

So what makes us tend toward one side or the other? Why are some parents too lenient while others give too many consequences? Our personalities play a huge role in our discipline, for better or for worse. I tend toward a control-freak personality. I don't struggle with consistency as much as I struggle with grace. Other moms might be free-spirited and laid-back, struggling with requiring respect and obedience from their kids.

Our past also plays a part in which extreme we lean toward. Some parents will seek to emulate how they were raised. Others will rebel against their own upbringing by raising their kids as differently as possible.

Our discipline can also be impacted by cultural pressure. What's the latest discipline research? What do popular psychologists say? Some parents feel immune to the world's opinions on discipline, but we can't forget about the impact of church culture. What are other Christian parents doing? How do we measure up with our peers within the church? Whatever nudges us toward one direction or the other on the scale, we need to be aware of what these two extremes look like and how to avoid them.

Too Much

Considering the gospel-based definition for discipline that we've already discussed, there really is no way to discipline *too much*. Discipline means shepherding hearts, training minds, and cultivating a loving relationship with our kids that points them to Christ. So, when we talk about too much discipline here, we are referring to harshness or consequences that don't quite fit the crime. This errs on the side of punishment, which we have seen is very different from discipline. By its very definition, discipline is the opposite of harshness.

When I was in college, I attended a Bible study led by a young dad. During one of our studies, he tearfully shared with the group that he felt like he had blown it with his son. "I have been too harsh with him," he said. His son was only three years old, and this dad realized that his expectations of him were not realistic. He desperately wanted to raise his son to love God. But, coming from an unbelieving home himself, he parented in reaction against his own upbringing. He hadn't been disciplined as a child, and he wanted something different for his son. He wanted to protect his son from all the things he had gotten away with as a child. He overreacted by disciplining his son too often and too harshly.

Overreacting always throws our discipline off balance. We might overreact against our own lack of discipline, like my Bible study leader. We might also overreact out of anger, fatigue, or embarrassment. Overreacting comes from wanting certain results so badly we will do whatever it takes to get those results.

The gospel helps us to stop and reevaluate. It tells us to loosen our grip on those sought-after results and ask, "What does my child's heart need right now?" When my son has teased his brother for the fifth time in a row, my frustration tempts me to overreact. Gospel discipline stops me in my tracks and reminds me, "The goal isn't to make him stop at whatever cost. The goal is to address his heart, again and again, no matter how long it takes."

Another way to protect ourselves from disciplining too much is to discern the difference between disobedience and childishness. It is easy to confuse the two, because they often look very similar. Proverbs 22:15 tells us that foolishness is bound up in the heart of a child. Our kids have a natural inclination to disobey. But this verse doesn't negate the reality of developmental stages. My 12-month-old throws cereal across the kitchen out of curiosity. As I train him to keep his cereal on his tray, I have to remember that his foolishness is not always disobedience. It's a stage. Paul acknowledges these stages in 1 Corinthians 13:11 when he says, "When I was a child, I spoke like a child, I thought like a child, I reasoned like a child. When I became a man, I gave up childish ways." My son will not always throw cereal. One day he will be a man. No children, even if they are raised under consistent godly discipline, can skip these developmental stages. They must go through them. We can help them develop with love and patience while also showing them there are boundaries that keep them safe.

A final factor that contributes to going overboard is our desire to control. This is often rooted in our own insecurities. Remember my control-freak side that I mentioned? When I had my first baby I was afraid that, if I wasn't on top of every little thing he did, his natural foolishness would take over. I would lose him. The foolishness that is "bound up in the heart of a child" can be scary. What if we're not on top of it? What will happen if we accidentally let too many things slide? The solution is not rules piled on top of more rules. This is a quick way to burden our kids and dishearten them. The Bible warns against provoking or frustrating our kids (see Eph. 6:4). This verse goes on to say, "But bring them up in the discipline and instruction of the Lord." Frustrating their hearts is counterproductive to godly discipline.

If we let our desire to control our kids take over, we will lose sight of their hearts. Often, when I wake up in the morning, I lie in bed for an extra few seconds and pray, "Lord, help me to discipline each child according to his own heart today." If I'm not purposeful about loosening my grip on control, I will forget what it's all for. Do we want to control our kids, or do we want to shepherd them? Does their sin scare us into more rules, or does it bring us to our knees in prayer as we ask for more wisdom and love?

Too Little

Have you heard the expression "Choose your battles"? I've heard this phrase come up more often in parenting situations than in any other area of life. It means choosing what is a big deal and what's not. Unfortunately, sometimes we as parents use this phrase to opt out of discipline.

Consider this scenario: A mom pours her daughter some cereal in a blue bowl. She sets it down in front of her. The little girl screams in anger and pushes it away. "I want the *pink* bowl!" she screams, scowling and wildly kicking her legs under the table. The mom glances inside the cupboard. Yes, there is a pink bowl there. Sighing, the mom thinks to herself, *I have to choose my battles,* and she gets the pink bowl out of the cupboard and re-pours the cereal.

We've all been in similar situations. We're tired. We want to make our kids happy. We think, *I'll discipline my child when he does something really bad.* If we continue with the analogy of a battle, we can see how dangerous this thinking is. Imagine walking onto a real battlefield. The enemy comes rushing toward you. You're seconds away from being face-to-face with your foe. You don't have the option of saying "I don't feel like fighting today" or "The enemy doesn't look that strong. I'll fight when a bigger enemy comes along." We don't get to choose whether or not we will battle our kids' sin. We enter into the battle the day we become parents.

It's important to remember we are never fighting *against* our own children. We are fighting alongside them. When we lay down our swords, we expose our kids to attack. They are too young to fight for themselves. We have to do battle *for* them. Doing battle with sin means getting our hands dirty. It means fighting for our kids' hearts even when we're too tired.

What would it have looked like if the mom in the scenario above had picked up her sword? She might have said, "That was not a respectful way to ask for the pink bowl. Please try again." Or she could have said, "You may not have the pink bowl today because I want you to practice being thankful for what you have. When you show me thankfulness, you will be allowed to have more choices." Perhaps that's where the discipline would end. But even if the mom knew it would only make her daughter angrier, requiring still more discipline, sin is always a battle worth fighting.

So which battles can we choose? Does every interaction with our kids have to end in discipline? We have to confront discipline situations when they arise, but there are times we can avoid confrontation before it starts.

I was at a friend's house one day, and she told her three-year-old daughter to go get her jacket. Her daughter ran the other way. My friend sighed. She was in a hurry to leave, but she knew what she had to do. "I have to discipline her now," she said. "I should have just gotten her jacket myself!" My friend could have gotten the jacket herself instead of asking her daughter to do it. But once a direct command was given, it had to be obeyed. That doesn't mean she should always get her daughter's jacket just because her daughter might disobey. Sometimes we can look for ways to avoid conflict with our kids, but not always. While we never want to make unnecessary rules, we also can't make our lives revolve around avoiding conflict with our kids. Regardless, if a conflict is already in progress, we have to deal with it. If we opt out in the middle of it, we leave our kids alone on the battlefield.

Too little discipline means being unwilling or unprepared to do battle with our kids' sin. It means not requiring the obedience that God requires. When we discipline too little, we sacrifice giving our kids the gospel. This might sound extreme, but let's look at two ways that we see this in Scripture.

First, we sacrifice the gospel by misrepresenting God to our kids. I talked to one mom recently who said that she didn't give her little ones consequences because she wants to be gracious to them like God is gracious to her. It is true that God "does not deal with us according to our sins, nor repay us according to our iniquities" (Ps. 103:10). But that is only because our debt was paid by another. If we want to know how God feels about sin, we need to look at the cross. The gruesome, bloody death of our Savior shows us how ugly sin is. Our discipline will point our kids to the cross, too. When we discipline them, we remind them how God feels about sin. We remind them that he is holy and deserves our obedience. It is only then that the grace of the gospel can truly shine. It's a beautiful chain reaction: the holiness of God shows us our sin, which shows us our need of a savior. When we don't discipline, we take away the first link in the chain, and the need for a savior disappears.

A lack of discipline also breaks down relationship—both between our kids and us and between our kids and God. The mom's comment about God's graciousness is ironic, because she was equating grace with no consequences. The Bible tells us the exact opposite. Everyone whom God loves "he disciplines, and he scourges every son whom he receives" (Heb. 12:6 NASB). It is not gracious to withhold discipline from our kids. Proverbs 13:24 even tells us it is hateful.

In the short term, it can feel like discipline hurts our relationships with our kids. They might get angry with us and make us feel like the bad guy. But God has given us the big picture. Discipline is a long-term commitment meant for a long-term relationship. The love and protection that we give our kids through discipline mimics the relationship that God has with us. Every time we lovingly discipline our kids, we put another sign on the road map that points them to God. When we don't discipline, the way is unclear. Their relationship to God is foggy.

So how do we strike that gospel balance with our discipline—the balance that shows loving authority and grace at the same time? This is where wisdom comes in. The Bible is not a reference book that gives us a play-by-play for every discipline situation we can imagine. Every parent has a different personality, and so does every child. With that in mind, let's take a look at a side-by-side comparison of the two discipline extremes.

Scenario #1: Your son hits his friend at the park.

Too much: You hurry your son back to the car. As soon as you are safely inside and out of the earshot of the other moms, you yell at your son for embarrassing you and tell him he is never coming back to the park again.

Too little: You stay seated on the bench and say, "Keep your hands to yourself." Not sure whether or not he even heard you,

you shrug and say to the other moms next to you, "Kids will be kids."

Gospel balance: You call your son over to you to make sure he has your attention. You calmly say, "That was not loving, and it did not show self-control. Go apologize to your friend and then sit here with me until I tell you that you can get up and play."

Scenario #2: You call your daughter to come to dinner, and she says "No!"

Too much: You discipline her with harshness and take away dinner. You give her a punishment but no chance to practice a correct response.

Too little: You think to yourself, *Maybe she's just not hungry. I know I don't like to eat when I'm not hungry, so I don't want to impose that on her.* You let her continue to play until she feels like coming.

Gospel balance: You realize this is about her heart, not her appetite. You tell your daughter that her answer was not acceptable, and you give her the appropriate consequence. You teach your daughter the right response, telling her that saying yes to Mom is saying yes to God. You give her a chance to practice a proper response.

God's Word, prayer, and a commitment to consistent discipline will give us wisdom to find the balance in each situation.

Reflection

1. Do you lean more toward too much or too little discipline? What about your personality or your past experiences has influenced you?

2. Look up Proverbs 13:24. *How* does this verse say we should discipline? How does this help us keep the balance between too much and too little?

3. How would you explain the difference between childishness and disobedience?

4. Ephesians 6:4 tells us not to "provoke," or frustrate, our kids. We've seen how too much discipline can do this. How can not enough discipline also frustrate our kids?

6

From Emotion-Led to Spirit-Led Discipline

We've seen that intentionality can be our insurance against disciplining too much or too little. When we take time to evaluate our kids' hearts, we are more likely to make a balanced decision in our discipline. Now we're going to see how the enemy of an intentional response is an emotional response. Our emotions can be a great asset to our discipline, but only if we submit them to the Holy Spirit. That's the difference between heartfelt discipline and simply flying off the handle. As we seek to strike the gospel balance between too much and too little, we need to understand the subtle differences between being led by the Spirit and being led by our emotions.

Nothing pricks that sensitive place in our mommy hearts like disobedience. When our kids disobey, we're immediately tossed back and forth between disappointment, sadness, anger, and frustration. It's exhausting. But the fact that disobedience evokes emotion is not a bad thing. It means that your heart is in it. If your kids disobey and it *doesn't* faze you, take time to evaluate where your heart is. How important is their spiritual growth to you? Do you consider the effects that unchecked sin will have in the long run? Do you believe that their disobedience, as Hebrews 12:6 says, requires action on your part in order to show love to your children?

God's Word calls us to invest our hearts in discipline. Emotions are bound to be part of this. Our emotions will inevitably be stirred up, but we can't let emotions rule our discipline. Why? Our emotions are not always sanctified—meaning that they are often rooted in self-centeredness rather than what's in the best interest of our kids. Without realizing it, I often take my kids' disobedience personally. It becomes all about me. I feel disrespected, inconvenienced, and (when we're out in public) embarrassed. It feels like a personal failure. I feel like I've invested time and energy into this and deserve some payoff.

So what part should emotions play in our discipline? First, it's helpful to look at the two extremes we want to avoid.

Too Objective

If you are afraid of disciplining in anger, you might take the approach of trying to remove your emotions altogether. You don't trust yourself. You want to turn discipline into a mathematical formula in order to protect your own heart from the painful emotions.

I talked to a mom recently who had a very detailed spanking system for certain offenses. Each offense had a certain number of spankings attached to it. For example, lying was seven swats, back talk was three, hitting a sibling was four, and so on. When I asked her how it was working, she shook her head and sighed. "Well, one day my son did three things on the list all at the same time. He hit his sister, lied about it, and then talked back to me. So I took him to the spanking chart, and we did the math together. He got fourteen swats."

Her system left out one key element: the Holy Spirit. Biblical discipline is not a giant calculator that we plug a formula into and out comes the answer. As much as we would like to simplify discipline down to a formula, we can never take the shepherding part out of it. If discipline boiled down to nothing more than mathematical calculations, we wouldn't need wisdom from God's Word and the Holy Spirit. While we can't take for granted the importance of consistency, we also need to leave room for the Holy Spirit to guide us. Purely objective discipline says, "What does my discipline chart say?" Spirit-led discipline says, "What does my child's heart need right now?"

To evaluate whether or not we are being too objective, we can look at the picture of a shepherd. "He will tend his flock like a shepherd; he will gather the lambs in his arms; he will carry them in his bosom, and gently lead those that are with young" (Isa. 40:11). The picture of this shepherd is one of ultimate tenderness. That doesn't mean discipline is not part of the picture. Shepherds carry a long staff. The staff is used to guide the sheep, sometimes painfully, away from danger. But there is an element of gentleness here. There is a personal relationship that takes into account many different factors. The mom who I talked to was hyperfocused on the actual offenses and what they deserved. Perhaps she was blinded to the actual offender, her son, and what his heart needed. Yes, he might have still needed a spanking. But if our kids rack up a consequence that is almost too big to bear, we have to ask ourselves what our objective is. Are we simply helping them pay off a debt? What picture do we paint of God when our discipline has this objective?

Recently a friend asked me if it was okay to hug her toddler after a spanking. "I'm afraid I might be sending him mixed messages," she said. She thought that emotions and discipline were so incompatible that it was safer not to mix the two. And to that question, I say yes! Hug your kids. Hug them all day long. A shepherd hugs. Giving discipline without that sweet intimacy is what sends mixed messages. It tells our kids, "Mommy loves me, but only when I'm good." It's okay for our kids to see our brokenness and even our displeasure over their sin. It makes our willingness to discipline them the ultimate act of love, not retribution.

I vividly remember a time my husband gave our toddler a spanking. My husband immediately hugged him, and our sweet little boy cupped his daddy's face with his chubby hands and kissed his cheek while he cried. They comforted each other. Even at such a young age, he soaked up the love that went hand in hand with the discipline. He knew that Daddy was doing something difficult for him out of love. If we are too objective, we will lose tenderness. If we lose tenderness, we will miss a chance to point our kids to the gospel.

Too Emotional

If we go to the opposite extreme and discipline out of emotion, our feelings become more important than what our kids need. We trade teachable moments for blowups. We trade shepherding for letting off steam.

It's impossible to be consistent if you discipline solely based on your emotions. Growing up, I had a close friend who was raised by emotional discipline. Every day, her mom's standards changed based on her mood—but she still expected her daughter to obey no matter what. Her daughter grew up frustrated and rebellious. She felt like she could do no right by her mom—so why even try? In the end she lost respect for her mom. Her mom's actions showed that her ultimate authority was her own feelings rather than God's Word. Blowups might accomplish your goal in the short term, but they build resentment in the long run.

If you had to pick one emotion that threatens to take over your discipline, what would it be? For myself, and I think for many parents, the answer is easy: anger. Anger itself is not necessarily sinful—especially when we are angry at sin. But it turns sinful very quickly when we use it to justify disciplining too harshly. If we're honest with ourselves, our anger is rarely righteous. It is usually fueled by hurt pride or a sense of personal offense. John Piper says, "We should get angry with sin, but that anger should be so mingled with heart-sorrows for the people sinning."[1] Anger at sin fuels compassion toward the sinner.

When I measure God's response to my own sin against how I respond to my kids' sin, his compassion puts me to shame. "The LORD is merciful and gracious, slow to anger and abounding in steadfast love" (Ps. 103:8). If I am truly angry at my kids' sin, I will be extra compassionate in my discipline. That doesn't mean backing down from consequences, but it does mean keeping them in perspective. I can ask, "Is this just to help me let off steam, or am I purposefully seeking after my child's heart?" Yelling, threatening, and harshness are all about me. I want my discipline to revolve around my kids. I need to discipline in a way that directly benefits them.

No matter how justified we might feel in our angry outbursts, we have to remember that anger does not "achieve the righteousness of God" (James 1:20 NASB). Anger goes back to punishment rather than discipline. It seeks retribution, not reconciliation. It demands personal satisfaction and justice. If we choose to seek those things, we will do so at the cost of shepherding.

What Can You Do with Your Emotions?

How do we strike the balance between being too objective and too emotional? The balance is struck when we allow the Holy Spirit to guide our discipline *in* our emotions. We don't remove our emotions from the equation, but we also don't give them free rein. When I'm tempted to let my emotions call the shots, these are the practical strategies that I turn to.

Mommy Time-Out

I took a sewing class in high school. My teacher (who also happened to be my mother) always reminded the class to "measure twice, cut once." The point is that you can consider your options for as long as you want, but you can only act once. Once you discipline your child, you can't take it back. When the emotion first hits, think twice before you discipline. Give yourself a minute in the bathroom, even if chaos is still ensuing right outside the door. Step back, take anger out of the equation, and see whether the consequence should still be the same. Perhaps it should be. But now it will be done in love rather than anger.

I was not prepared for the stress that three babies under the age of three would bring. In the beginning years of becoming a mom, I often handled the stress by yelling and flying off the handle. I would cry myself to sleep wishing I could do the whole day over and give my precious babies the calm, loving mommy they deserved. God used those painful moments to create a new perspective in my heart. I began to stare stress in the face and say, "Whatever I do now I can't take back. How will I feel when I'm tucking my kids into bed tonight? When the stress is gone and I'm kissing their sleeping faces, will I be filled with painful regrets or will I be able to laugh at the craziness of this day?" That perspective has been life changing for me. I still don't handle stress perfectly, but by God's grace I am in a different place now than I was when I first became a mom.

Look at the Clock

I have heard this strategy from several different friends, and I love it. When total chaos is consuming your house and you feel like you are about to lose it, look at the clock. Tell yourself, "I can have a meltdown in ten minutes." Then take a deep breath and simply survive the next ten minutes. Things change so quickly. By the time ten minutes go by, there is a good chance that the kids will be occupied with something else, you will feel calmer, and your discipline strategy (if you even still need one) will be clearer. The goal is that you won't actually need to have a meltdown. I'm amazed at how fast things change in my home. Total calm can turn into a raging storm within seconds, and vice versa. If I respond to the storm within the first few seconds, peace might have been on its way, but now I have left a trail of hurt feelings and misjudged discipline to deal with. Ten minutes is often all it takes to see a complete turnaround in my home.

Whisper

Yelling is like letting water out of a dam. It's the doorway that lets all your anger and frustration come flooding out. Even as you hear yourself doing it, you can't seem to stop. When you feel the yell coming, take a deep breath and whisper. It has a twofold effect: it immediately helps to diffuse your anger while also causing your kids to listen better because they have to lean in and concentrate on what you're saying. If your kids are used to hearing you yell, this will be a fascinating change for them—worth paying attention to!

It is hard to parent from a distance. If your child is disobeying you and you are on the other side of the room, emotions will escalate. You feel more out of control. You feel like you have to yell. Take the time to stop what you're doing, get up, and go to your child. Make direct eye contact and talk in a soft, clear voice.

Pray

You might not feel like you have the time or the right frame of mind to pray in the middle of an emotional discipline situation. But we have to remember what prayer is: communication with God. It doesn't require a certain place, certain words, or a perfectly peaceful frame of mind. In the Psalms we can see that David's prayers were often "God, help!"

I love the expression *arrow prayers*. I shoot up arrow prayers all day long. As soon as I hear the screams and I know I am about to come face-to-face with a discipline situation, I say, "Lord, help me." In that brief half second, I am reminded who is ultimately in control. I'm reminded who I answer to as I go to administer discipline to the children he gave me. I'm reminded that his strength is sufficient to help me discipline. I don't have to supplement it with anger.

Debrief

After the moment has passed, evaluate your reaction. Were you able to control your emotions, or did they control you? What was the root of your anger? What worked, and what didn't work, to diffuse your emotions? Were you able to communicate love in your discipline? What could go better next time? Is there anything you need to apologize to your kids for? Perhaps your child did need the discipline, but if you believe that you disciplined out of anger, it's appropriate to tell your child, "You needed a spanking because what you did was wrong, but I should have talked to you in a gentle way. I'm sorry my words were not gentle. Do you forgive me?"

68

Reflection

1. What are the dangers of making our discipline too objective?
2. Read Ephesians 4:31–32. According to these verses, which emotions should be a regular part of our discipline and which ones shouldn't?
3. According to the last phrase of Ephesians 4:32, what should be our motive in disciplining with compassion?
4. Explain how discipline and tenderness can work with each other rather than against each other.

7

Setting Our Expectations

Yesterday I had a standoff with a three-year-old. I had just told him to sit on the couch and think about how he could be gentler with his little brother. He folded his arms and said, "I will *not* think about *anything.*" I was momentarily speechless. I wasn't used to him talking to me that way. He was a pretty laid-back kid. And, after all, that kind of disrespect is *not* part of our home. He should know better . . . shouldn't he?

I had to catch myself. No, he does not know better. He, like all of us, was born with a sinful heart. If gone unchecked, that sin in his heart is ready to show itself at unexpected times. I also had to remind myself that that kind of disrespect most certainly *is* part of our home—because our home is filled with sinners. In order to discipline effectively I have to expect my kids to sin—often.

Requiring vs. Expecting

There is a difference between *requiring* obedience and *expecting* obedience. If we parent according to a biblical world-view of man's natural sinful condition, we actually expect our kids to rebel against our rules. It should come as no surprise when they disobey. We know what is in their hearts. But that doesn't mean we stop *requiring* them to obey. We set the boundaries, make the rules, and then stand ready to lovingly discipline when they disobey. We don't excuse their sin just because we know it is inevitable. Just the opposite! We prepare for it. What a blessing to have this insight into their hearts before they can even say their first word.

Scripture teaches that everyone is accountable to God's law—not just Christians. Romans 1:20 says that the whole world is "without excuse." In the Old Testament, the whole tribe of Israel was bound to obey God's law even though they were not all saved. We hold our kids to God's standards—not because we assume they are saved, but because we are teaching them something about God and about themselves. God is holy. We are not. God is all-powerful. We are dependent on him. Therefore, he deserves our obedience.

Our kids are not going to obey on their own. They need our help. When you look at your angelic, sleeping infant, it's easy to fall into the cultural mind-set that mankind is basically good. When that angel turns two, your philosophy of man's basic goodness goes down the toilet, along with your cell phone that the toddler just flushed. We want to discipline according to the gospel, not to culture. Gospel-centered discipline begins with the foundational truth that we are all sinners. Our children are born with a heart problem. God has given us, their parents, the job of training those hearts. When we acknowledge the reality of the battle we are fighting, we will pick up the right weapons.

When my three-year-old told me he would "*not* think about *anything*," he was not off the hook for his disrespectful answer—but, more importantly, neither was Mommy. I had a job to do. My son was doing what came naturally to him: disobeying. It was up to me to show him how to obey.

Most Christian parents would claim to have high standards of obedience for their children. It's easy to forget that the burden of those standards falls on us as the parents. *Requiring our kids to obey starts with requiring ourselves to do something about their disobedience.* They don't know any better. We do. If we don't expect our kids to disobey, we will be caught off guard when it happens and will respond in one of two ways: either we will become angry and frustrated by their misbehavior or we will be oblivious to it.

1. Anger and Frustration

Think about the last blowup you had at your kids. Most likely they had done something disobedient, destructive, or just plain foolish. I remember telling my six-year-old last week, in a moment of frustration, "I never thought to tell you not to cut my tube of toothpaste open with scissors. I can't make a rule about *everything*. You know what's right and what's wrong!" But, no, he doesn't. That's why he has Mom and Dad. We are his beacon in the darkness, showing him the way to life and peace. I need to be prepared, not angry. My training should always be done in gentleness and patience, with the knowledge that my son and I share the common problem of sin. If my Savior was tempted in all things as I am, so that he can show me grace (see Heb. 4:15), how could I not show that same grace to my son? That doesn't mean excusing sin, but it does mean handling it with gentleness.

When my kids speak to me disrespectfully, it catches me off guard. Being caught off guard is a recipe for anger. It causes us to take our kids' sin personally: "How dare he talk to me like that!" Our pride gets offended: "I don't deserve to be talked to like that." But their sin has nothing to do with us. Their sin is ultimately between them and God. If I respond in pride and anger, that is wrong. If I let them off the hook and think, *All kids go through this; they'll grow out of it,* that is also wrong. I am responsible to discipline my kids in order to show them their sin is an offense to a holy God, not to me. "Disobeying is not good for your heart," I tell them. "I love your heart, so I need to show you that what you said was wrong."

When I feel my frustration rising over my kids' disobedience, I remind myself that this is what I signed up for. Loving my kids doesn't just mean that I get to give them ice cream and kiss their cute faces all day. I get the mess, too. In that split second of anger, I tell myself, "This sin is all he knows right now. God has blessed him by placing him in a Christian home where he will come face-to-face with the gospel when he sins. Give him the gospel, not your anger." I'm amazed at how instantaneously that changes my attitude. Frustration vanishes. I feel compassion for my son, who is not really rebelling against me but against God. At the end of the discipline, I can say to the Lord, "It's up to you. I was faithful to discipline. I don't know whether it 'worked,' but I don't have to worry about that. It's in your hands."

2. Oblivious Parenting

If we don't expect our kids to disobey, then we won't notice it when it happens. At a birthday party a couple of years ago, I saw a mom tell her son not to eat any more cookies. She went back to talking to her friends—and he went right back to eating cookies. A week later, at church, I observed a similar situation. Except this time I was the oblivious parent who continued talking when my child was disobeying right under my nose (eating cookies, of course). I gave a direction and expected it to be obeyed, but one key element was missing: follow-through.

Do we sometimes expect our kids to obey, but don't expect ourselves to have to put forth the necessary effort to follow through? It happens when we forget to expect our kids to disobey. It would be nice if giving an order was enough, but it's not. We have to show our kids *how* to obey and be ready to show them what happens when they don't. We share a responsibility in their disobedience. Husband and wife authors Paul and Karen Tautges say that when we are too lazy to discipline, we absorb the shame of our kids' disobedience: "Though the little child is indeed guilty, at this point the greater shame belongs to us as parents who should know better and should love our child enough to train him or her to act properly. Otherwise, the wise observer may silently ask, 'What is wrong with that parent?'"[1]

God's Word confirms this in Proverbs 29:15: "The rod and reproof give wisdom, but a child left to himself brings shame to his mother." This verse isn't saying we are responsible for their sin, but it shows how connected we are to it. God has given us a job, and he expects us to be faithful. If we are not intentional about discipline, we can expect the shame that comes with not being faithful.

These are training years. We are in the trenches. Yes, we will miss out on conversations with our friends. We may have to suddenly hang up the phone or pull over the car. We have to parent with the expectation that our kids will disobey, and it is up to us to step in immediately and train them. Obedience does not happen naturally.

There is a beautiful parallel between God's parenting and our parenting. God knows we are sinners, but he does not treat us as our sins deserve, because we are his beloved children (see Ps. 103:10). However, if he let our sin go unchecked, he would not be a loving Father. He disciplines out of love (see Heb. 12:6). When we expect our kids to disobey, we are able to strike that balance of grace and discipline. We should not get angry and frustrated, but we must also not become passive.

This is why God has blessed us moms with the supernatural ability to have eyes in the backs of our heads. Do we use them? Are we aware of what our kids are doing, or are we too focused on getting that next project done? It's so easy to get distracted. When I tell my son to clean up his room, I can go back to folding laundry, but I have to make a conscious decision to keep an ear open. The Bible tells me that my tenderhearted boy is still young and foolish and needs accountability (see Prov. 22:15). If I expect him to obey and never check on him, I will inevitably walk by his room an hour later and find that it's still a mess. I *expect* my son to clean his room when I tell him to, meaning that I have set standards and there will be consequences for disobeying. I also *expect* that he will need my follow-through in order to learn how to meet those standards successfully.

The Importance of Grace

Remember the beautiful gospel balance we are seeking to strike in our discipline? At this point we need to take a step back and evaluate what expecting our kids to disobey does *not* mean. It does not mean we hound our children all day and wait for them to mess up. It does not mean that we constantly assume the worst about them. Disobedience is central to the gospel story, but so is grace. If we hyperfocus on one, we will sacrifice the other. We can go overboard in treating our kids as if they're always "up to something." We will automatically blame them for things. If our kids feel like they can do no right by us, they won't be motivated to try. If our actions communicate that we don't trust them, they will not aspire to trustworthiness.

One of my kids struggles with rudeness more than his brothers do. I can remind him a thousand times a day to say, "Please," "thank you," "excuse me," and so on, and the next day I will have to remind him a thousand times again. Recently, when it seemed like there had been no improvement, I decided I needed a new approach. Instead of correcting him every time he was rude, I watched intently for ways to praise him. It was difficult. I had to let a few obvious opportunities for correction slide, but I wanted to give him a chance. Sure enough, in the midst of all of his regular rudeness, I heard him say "Excuse me" when he shoved past his brother. I grabbed him and hugged him and said, "I heard you! That's exactly what we've been practicing, isn't it? You are being kind like Jesus. I am so proud of you." My son was so surprised and giddy at my reaction. He couldn't believe he had actually done it right. He immediately looked around for something else polite he could do. I was struck by what an impression my encouragement left on him. Just as he was always unaware of his rudeness, he was also unaware of when he had done something right. In his immaturity, he still couldn't see a clear connection between my instruction and his actions. He needed me to point it out to him.

In our family, the dinner table is the natural place to review the events of the day. I often use that time to tell each child a specific way that he obeyed well. On difficult days filled with discipline and growing pains, I really have to dig for something. But my kids need to know that I see them when they obey, not just when they disobey. The eyes in the back of my head aren't just for catching my kids when they disobey, but also for catching them when they do obey.

I became a Christian when I was very young. At various points in my Christian journey, I have thought to myself, *I seem to be getting* more *sinful. What's going on?* In reality, as I get to know my Savior better, I begin to see my sin more clearly. As soon I address one issue in my life, God shows me another. It is one of God's great mercies that he does not reveal all our sin to us at once. We would be too burdened, too discouraged. Instead he allows us to see little victories along the way, giving us fresh strength to put sin to death in our lives.

Our kids need to see *their* little victories. We can easily burden them if we only highlight their weaknesses. As we gear up to handle their disobedience, we need to be equally equipped to praise and encourage them.

We have been teaching our kids catechism. Question 11 of the *Catechism for Young Children* says, "Q: Can you see God? A: No—I cannot see God, but he can always see me."[2] Teaching our kids to glorify a God they cannot see can be difficult. He does not give them a pat on the back when they obey. They don't hear a "Good job!" from God when no one is around and they decide not to touch the plate of cookies on the table. God has given them *us*. They need to hear our words of affirmation. We can help give them a tangible picture of what it means to glorify God—which means we must be vigilant about catching them doing good.

I'm a terrible bowler. I've had a few strikes in my lifetime, but I've had more gutter balls than I can count. Our kids are like bowling balls rolled by a bad bowler. They are all over the lane. Our discipline is like the big, rubber bumper strips that keep the ball from going in the gutter. As they go through the day, our kids naturally head toward those gutters over and over again. Our discipline nudges them back into the lane, reminding them, "I'm still here. This is my job. I know you'll be headed for this edge many times today, but I'm not going to let you fall in." We expect our kids to sin, and we also expect that they will need lots of encouragement along the way.

Reflection

1. How does a biblical perspective on your child's natural sinfulness help you avoid frustration?

2. In the same way, how does a biblical perspective on your child's natural sinfulness inspire you to have better follow-through and not be an "oblivious parent"?

3. How would our culture react to the claim that our kids are naturally sinful? How has a cultural view of children impacted parenting in today's society?

4. When was the last time you caught your child doing good? Think of a specific area of disobedience that your child struggles with. How can you purposefully look for ways to catch your child doing good in this area?

Part 2

PRACTICAL TOOLS

How Does It Really Look?

8

Daily Structure: Why Routine Is Essential

I've played paintball only once in my life, and I hated it. I don't have an ounce of tomboy in me, which is probably why God blessed me with five little boys. Paintball was terrifying to me. I never knew when or where a painful sting would hit, followed by the splat of neon goo. By the end of the game I was shaking, and I was covered with hits.

Isn't that exactly how we mamas often feel at the end of a "discipline day"? You know what I mean. The bullets start flying first thing in the morning. The toddler chucks his breakfast on the floor. The four-year-old hits his brother. The oldest decides to enter teenage rebellion at age six. Every discipline situation is like an unexpected, painful hit from out of nowhere. But there's good news. Discipline doesn't have to feel like a losing paintball battle. There is a foundational tool that makes discipline predictable and productive: *structure*.

Before you cringe and stop reading, let me put your mind at ease. Structure doesn't mean rigid rules and schedules that add more pressure to your day just to leave you feeling like a failure at the end of it. Structure simply means having a plan. It means that your day has consistency and purpose.

Some moms thrive on spontaneity and find structure to be burdensome. If that describes you, don't worry. I'm not going to try to force you into a mold that doesn't fit your personality. Instead, I want to help you find practical ways to provide a firm foundation for your kids. During the child-raising years, things change on a daily basis. What are our constants? What can our kids predict and depend on? These are the areas that give us time to teach and train.

Every piece of structure in our day, each unchangeable that our kids can depend on, is a pit stop on the racetrack. It's where we refuel, talk, practice, and refresh our kids' hearts before sending them back to the race.

I was talking to a new mom recently. She said, "I was so laid-back before I had a baby. I didn't have any schedule or routine. Now I feel like I have to have a routine for everything!" She was referring to things like sleeping schedules, feeding schedules, and regular diaper changes. Having a baby forces some women to seriously consider schedules for the first time. If you didn't feed her, change her, or put her to sleep regularly, your baby would not get what she needed. As babies grow, they continue to need predictability and consistency in order to learn the discipline that their hearts need.

On the other hand, babies throw structured women into sudden unpredictability. You can't predict when a toddler will get the stomach flu. You can't plan when and where your child will have a meltdown. You can't depend on how much sleep you will get each night.

Whether you naturally gravitate toward structure or not, structure is possible for every mom. That's because there are as many varieties of structure as there are moms. No matter how our daily routines vary from one another's, we can still share the same goal: creating an environment of consistency in which to teach and train.

Structure is crucial to the mental and spiritual development of our kids. It gives them ample time and a secure environment to practice the skills we teach them. If you wanted your child to learn piano, you would have him sit at the piano and practice. That's structure. If you didn't have any structure, it would be like having him learn to play the piano by hitting a key or two every time he ran through the room. No consistency plus no plan equals no learning. In the same way, successful discipline doesn't happen without some sort of structure.

Structure can be as simple as intentionality. What do you do intentionally with your kids each day? We see how training and structure go hand in hand in Deuteronomy 11:19. This verse answers the question of when we are to teach our kids God's Word: "When you are sitting in your house, and when you are walking by the way, and when you lie down, and when you rise." There is intentionality and consistency.

I want to give you an example of my daily structure. Every mom's structure will look different. Mine is just one example. This is what I do with my five boys, who are aged seven and younger. The key to a daily structure is consistency. These are the things that we do at the same time, in the same place, and in the same way every day. You'll see the discipline skills I am able to plug into each phase of my structure.

- *Wake up.* The kids wake up around seven. They are allowed to get out of bed and play quietly in their rooms until seven thirty. The big boys have a digital clock they can read. They tell the little ones when it is seven thirty. I know some moms who use clocks that change color or

85

light up when it's time to get out of bed. My kids also have a CD player so they can turn on an audio story like *Little House on the Prairie*. This time slot gives my kids a chance to practice *thoughtfulness* and *self-control*. They are not allowed to wake up a sleeping brother, and they are not allowed to leave their rooms. If they don't follow these rules, they have to get back in their beds. I try to use this time for my Bible reading and coffee with my husband.

- *Breakfast.* Our kids have the same breakfast every day: cereal and scrambled eggs. I don't say, "What do you feel like having today?" This is my chance to teach *thankfulness* and *contentment*. If they complain about what I put in front of them, I take it away and say, "If you don't want your breakfast, you can say 'No thank you, Mommy,' and you may be excused. If you want your breakfast, you say 'Thank you, Mommy.'" When they know those are their only two options, they always choose thankfulness. We always have a special breakfast on Saturday, like pancakes or waffles.

- *Free play.* This is when the kids can choose an activity from the toy closet. They must clean up one before choosing another. We call this "free play" to remind them that freedom is a privilege. If they use their free play inappropriately (by causing a fight, being too wild, or not treating their toys responsibly), their freedom gets taken away, and I will choose an activity for them—usually sitting on their beds alone with a quiet toy or book. This teaches *wisdom* and *responsibility*. They have to practice making wise choices in order to protect their free time. This is also the time I look for opportunities to reinforce *kindness* as they interact with each other.

- *School.* This is our Bible time and general school routine. I get the older three started on independent work while I pull each child aside for individual work with me. We talk a lot about *endurance* during the school day and relate schoolwork to the work that they will do one day as men.
- *Outside time.* This time covers the same skills as free play. Since we do it every single day, they know it is non-negotiable. When I say, "Outside time!" everyone grabs their shoes and heads for the back door. They may not come back in until I tell them. In the wintertime, this switches to basement or bedroom time.
- *Lunch.* "Table behavior" gives the kids a chance to practice *self-control* and *politeness.* There is no playing, touching, loud sounds, or chewing and talking with their mouths open. Of course these things *do* happen at each meal, which is why it's the perfect opportunity for them to practice these rules. Actually, I just had to add one today: no licking someone else's face. The rules evolve as my kids show me new things they need to work on. We keep the rules repetitive and simple, and we talk about them throughout the entire meal.
- *Cleanup and quiet time.* Cleanup teaches *perseverance* and *responsibility.* All our toy bins are labeled, and they are always kept in the same place. This helps the kids not to feel overwhelmed when it's time to clean up. We model how to clean up around the time that the kids start walking. Quiet time is the same every day: twenty-five minutes of reading books quietly, twenty-five minutes of playing quietly in their rooms, and then twenty-five minutes of screen time. The little ones sleep during this time. My seven-year-old likes to leave his room and ask for different options. I say, "No. This is what we do every

day so I can teach you to have a *good attitude* and be *independent*." I started using a timer for him in his room so that he doesn't keep asking me if quiet time is over.

- *Separate play.* I tuck this in throughout the day in order to give each boy some space. Each has a different area to play in quietly. Some of my boys thrive on playing alone, and others hate it. I use this time to talk to them about *peace*. Sometimes it's okay to be alone with your thoughts, play quietly, and be creative. We say, "Our house is a house of peace, not chaos."

- *Bedtime.* The day continues with another block of free play, followed by dinner and our bedtime routine. The kids take turns in the bathroom getting ready for bed. As soon as each boy is done, he waits on his bed and quietly looks at books. When all the boys are ready for bed, we see whose turn it is to pick the book for me to read aloud. I have a "name block" that I turn each night to see whose turn it is. This eliminates fighting over who chooses. It also cuts down on "One more story!" They know it's one story every night. Sometimes we take a break from picture books and spend a few weeks on a chapter book. Right now, Daddy is reading them *Pilgrim's Progress*.

You can see that I plan out chunks of time, not every second. This gives me flexibility within my structure. You can also see that our day is very simple. It looks like we're just accomplishing basic survival. We're eating, playing, and picking up toys. But purposeful training is also happening. Structure frees up my brain to concentrate on the teachable moments that pop up within each activity.

What about moms who work outside the home? How can they implement structure in order to create shepherding moments? I have a good friend who works full-time. She drops her two daughters off at school and then goes to work. She describes her daily structure as a bit chaotic. Everyone gulps down their breakfast in the morning, and she doesn't plan dinner until she is driving home at the end of the day. Her special moments of shepherding revolve around bedtime. Every night, she and her husband get the girls ready for bed. They talk about the day and take their time putting on jammies and picking stuffed animals. Then Mommy climbs into bed with them one at a time, and they whisper and cuddle until the kids fall asleep. What precious times!

In direct contrast, I keep bedtime short and sweet in our home. After being home with the kids all day, I don't feel the need to draw it out. This is just one example of how structure might look different for working moms and stay-at-home moms. The common factors are intentionality and consistency. *When* and *how* are we regularly pursuing our kids' hearts? This can be sprinkled throughout the day or can take place in more concentrated chunks. But we have to make sure it's happening.

What about playdates, family outings, and sicknesses? What happens when structure is interrupted? Think of your kids like Jell-O and your structure like those fancy Jell-O molds. Every day, you pour discipline and character training into your kids. Your structure is what holds it all together. Then, on special occasions when the structure is taken away, discipline still holds its shape. My kids know that behavior at a birthday party should be no different than behavior at home. The same thoughtfulness and self-control that they practice every day at home applies to walking around the grocery store.

Structure gives me time to keep our home a hospitable place for when guests drop in unexpectedly. Structure also helps our family to be able to say yes to ministry opportunities because we are more likely to be caught up on our own responsibilities. We teach our kids that we want to use our home for God's glory. Our structure helps us to be wise with our time and resources so that we have more to share with others. Having a predictable schedule for the kids protects my time as well as theirs, so that we have more time to do the things that are important to us.

As a blogger, I like to share with other moms whenever I discover a new tool that helps me with my structure. Moms sometimes ask me what *I* do during each phase of the kids' structure. The answer depends on what stage I'm at in developing our structure. When I first begin a new structure, it requires my constant hands-on involvement. I have to walk my kids through every step. I don't get much else done besides training, training, training. But once the structure becomes a habit, it frees up my time to do other things.

I use each phase of our daily structure to accomplish something for the home or family. While the kids go through their routine, I do my cleaning, meal prep, cooking, and responding to emails. But I have to be ready to stop what I'm doing at a moment's notice. My ears and eyes are doing double duty. Shepherding their hearts still has to be my priority. I often get wrapped up in a project, and then I find that I've missed opportunities to shape those discipline skills. Their routine is meant ultimately to benefit them, not to give me lots of free time.

Still not sure where to begin implementing structure? When I had my first baby, I was lost. He didn't follow any of the "rules" the books told me he would. I thought, *I'm all over the place! I have no idea what I'm doing, when I'm doing it, or how to make my day more structured for the sake of my family.* My first attempt to remedy this was to look online at all the organized, creative mamas I admired. I picked one of their daily routines and tried to make it my own. Big mistake. I realized that I couldn't copy someone else's routine. I could imitate their principles, but I had to make the routine my own.

My next attempt worked much better. I started by keeping a log of what I did with my baby each day. I wrote down every time I fed him, every time I put him to bed, and every time he woke up. I kept track of when we went on outings, when I did laundry, and when I prepped meals. After a couple of days, I looked over my notes, and I couldn't believe how structured my day already was. I used my existing structure as my baseline and improved on it by becoming more consistent. As I've had more babies and my kids have gotten older, I've been able to add more and more productivity to our daily structure.

My hope is that this has taken the intimidation out of structure for you. It is not meant to add more work to your plate. Remember how much energy it takes to dodge flying paintballs all day? Structure arms you. You go into quiet time thinking, *This is when we are going to practice self-control.* You go into free play thinking, *This is when I'm watching for those wise choices and kindness.* You're prepared. The day goes by faster and more smoothly. This is called "paying it forward." We invest our time and energy into structure and discipline now, and we will reap the benefits for years to come.

Reflection

Think about your daily structure. Jot down the things you do regularly in each chunk of time and evaluate which discipline skills you could incorporate into each phase. Add or change things that would help you to be more intentional about your day. Remember: too broad means not enough intentionality, and too detailed means setting yourself up for disappointment. Try to strike a balance between purposeful and realistic.

Phase of Day	Repetitive Activities	Discipline Skills
Wake-Up Routine		
Breakfast Hour		
Morning		
Lunch Hour		
Afternoon		
Dinner Prep Hour		
Dinner Hour		
Evening		
Bedtime Routine		

9

Words That Hurt, Words That Heal

I sat down at my friend's counter as she set out a big bowl of cherry tomatoes fresh from the garden. Her kids were a few years older than mine, and I was anxious to pick her brain about bad attitudes, politeness, and attentiveness to chores. As we snacked and talked, I slowly began to realize I was learning a lot more about myself as a mom than about my kids. We were talking about our words.

"I have a lecture for everything," she laughed. "No matter what the kids do or say, I have a speech ready. But I've learned that if lecturing is always my go-to response, I don't leave any room for the Holy Spirit. Now that my kids are older, I've tried to limit my instruction on most things to five words or less. Instead of a lecture on kindness or attitude, I say, 'Please use kind words.' Then I leave it there. I give the Holy Spirit a chance to do his work. If I realize later that they need more follow-up with my words, I give it."

I instantly related to what my friend was saying. Lately I have been struggling with my three-year-old. Whether it's obedience, potty training, or good manners, I feel like I lecture him from morning until bedtime. It's a tricky balance, because right now he needs my words to develop an understanding of all those things. But, if I'm not careful, my words can do more damage to his little heart than good.

We moms often compartmentalize yelling. We don't want to yell at our kids, so we work on controlling our tone and volume. But we don't consider other ways that our words can be hurtful. We need to take a step back and evaluate all our words, not just the words we yell. Some moms don't struggle with yelling, but their words can still be counterproductive to shepherding. Do we constantly pick at our children? Do we correct *every* fault all day long? Do we allow room for the Holy Spirit to do his work? Proverbs 12:18 says, "There is one whose rash words are like sword thrusts, but the tongue of the wise brings healing."

When I think about my three-year-old son, I want my words to bring healing to him. I've noticed that if I correct him too many times about too many things, his blue eyes lose their sparkle when they look at me. I get that glazed-over look that says, "Enough, Mommy. My heart can't absorb what you're saying—only that you are still not happy with me." Perhaps I'm not yelling; but, if my words aren't carefully measured with love and grace, they can be like sword thrusts.

In their little years, our kids need lots and lots of words. They don't know what kindness is. They don't know what self-control is, what good manners are, or why they even have to obey. We have to teach them. How can we be strategic about disciplining with our words?

Stories

My six-year-old is in the joke phase. He is finally figuring out how to tell a real joke, and it thrills him. Lately he's been testing the fine line between joking and lying. He thinks that he's just being funny, but he needs guidance to know what's okay and what's not. I tried to explain it to him a few times, but it wasn't sticking. He kept doing it. My words got lengthier and firmer; it still wasn't clicking. I wanted to tread lightly here. He loves jokes. I wanted to keep them a positive thing for him while still giving important instruction. He wasn't purposely disobeying, but he didn't understand.

Finally, I told him about the boy who cried "wolf." My son loves stories, so he was on the edge of his seat. When I got to the end I said, "So all of his sheep got eaten by the wolf because nobody believed him that the wolf had come. He had joked about it too many times." My son's eyes were wide. I could tell that his tender heart considered losing all those sheep a grave consequence. It finally sank in. He's told many silly jokes, but he hasn't told a joke-lie since. And he has asked to hear that story again many, many times.

Have you ever had your child come up to you and say, "Mommy, can you please lecture me again? I love it!" I don't think so. But how many times do our kids hang on our words when we tell them stories? Jesus used stories to teach valuable lessons too. When a lawyer asked him who his neighbor was, Jesus responded with the story of the good Samaritan (see Luke 10:25–37). When great crowds gathered to hear him speak, he told the story of the sower and the seed (see Matt. 13:1–23). There were many times when Jesus corrected his followers with direct words about their actions; but many other times he responded with "Once there was a man . . ."

What a gentle, gracious, effective way to teach our kids. When we take the spotlight off their own failures for a moment and apply it to someone else, sometimes their hearts can absorb it better. Tell stories. They will remember the lessons forever.

Word Bundles

I loved my friend's advice of asking myself, "How can I say what I want in five words or less?" I can do the same thing with my little ones, but first I have to lay some groundwork. I have to take time to carefully develop the various character traits I am teaching my kids. As I teach them a godly habit, I look for a few short words I can use over and over to encapsulate the entire meaning. I call it *word bundling*. *Word bundling* is pulling together everything that the godly habit includes and tying it up with one simple phrase. It's like a code between you and your kids. It helps you hone in on the exact skills you want to teach while saving you from lecture mode.

For example, my little boys have trouble listening. Sometimes they don't want to stop moving long enough. My word bundle for listening is "Listen with your whole body." It's one simple phrase, but my kids know the long list of behaviors it covers. We started by breaking it down. What does *listen* mean? What does *whole body* mean? We spent time defining it and practicing it. "It means to look at Mommy with your eyes. It means to stop wiggling and making silly faces. It means to stand right in front of me, not far away. It means you don't move your eyes or your body until I am done talking to you, and your mouth stays quiet." We did some silly practicing. I had them wiggle around the room and make funny sounds until I said, "Listen with your whole body." Then they snapped to attention, their eyes staring at mine widely, their mouths closed, suppressing giggles.

Now, when I use this word bundle, they know exactly what I mean and I don't have to say anything else. Think about how much time this saves. If I didn't have this word bundle, every time I had to talk to them, it would sound like this: "Boys, I need to talk to you. Come stand in front of me, please. No, closer.

Now—who's talking? No talking when I'm talking. Hold still, please. I'm trying to tell you something. Look at my eyes. Where are you going? Stand here. No, right *here*. Where did your eyes go? Can you listen when you are wiggling? I don't think so." And on and on and on. But when I take the time to tie all of that training together into one bundle, all I have to say is "Listen with your whole body." It is always a work in progress, but I can expect much quicker obedience when I use word bundles. I also feel like I am not wearing away at their spirits with my constant words. If I use a word bundle and they don't respond, then we go back and discuss it in depth. But the word bundle at least gives them a chance to obey first.

Every phase of your daily structure can contain helpful word bundles. The names of each activity are word bundles themselves. When I say "quiet time," it encompasses an entire paragraph that I don't have to repeat every day. We had to practice all the things that quiet time is and all the things it is not. It took a lot of time, effort, and discipline. But now the practice is paying off. It still amazes me that when I say, "Everyone head to your rooms for quiet time," I can peek down the hall two minutes later and see four little boys sitting on their beds quietly reading books. Yes, they still need reminders here and there, but this has become our new norm. We do it at the same time in the same way every day, and the word bundle *quiet time* always means the same thing.

Your word bundles are meant to be nonnegotiable. They help to keep things consistent and objective. They keep you from constantly redefining your expectations based on how you feel. They create an understanding between you and your kids that you can both depend on. When I say, "Listen with your whole body," my kids and I fall back on the same definition. There are no surprises, no new expectations—and no opportunities for them to claim that they misunderstood what I meant.

Here are some examples of other word bundles that we use on a daily (and hourly) basis. When I say the word bundle on the left, everything on the right is supposed to pop into my kids' hearts and minds.

Word Bundle	What It Means
Be a peacemaker	Listen to your brother and think about what he is saying to you. What would make him happy? Tell him how you feel in a calm way. Don't come to Mom or Dad until you have used kind words and listened well.
Use your words	Fussing and screaming are not allowed. If someone is bothering you, you must say "Please stop" or "No, thank you." If you want a turn, you say, "Can I please have a turn when you're done?" If you want to do something different from what Mommy said, you don't *tell* Mommy what you are going to do, you *ask*.
Sit-down activity	You must choose a toy or a game that can only be played sitting down. No wrestling, running, jumping, or moving from room to room.
Make a wise choice	What would Mom or Dad say about your choice? How does your choice affect those around you? Are you considering others or just yourself?

Be a gentleman	(Usually at the table) Chew with your mouth closed; sit on your bottom; don't do anything that would make someone feel yucky; act like a big grown-up daddy.
Come to Mommy	Stop what you are doing immediately and come to Mommy, ready to listen with your whole body. You may not finish what you are doing first, and you may not ask questions until after you have obeyed and come to Mommy.

The goal is to use the word bundle on the left more and more and not have to rehash the definition on the right every time. You can reinforce the definition by drawing attention to good examples. "Wow; look how you are using your fork instead of your hands! You are being a gentleman!" That encouragement drives home the definition of "Be a gentleman" without a lecture.

Many families choose to use creative phrases and even made-up words. This can make it fun for the kids. I choose to keep all my word bundles straightforward, because I love it when my kids hear the pastor use one of our word bundles in church. Their ears perk up, and they look at me like he just used our secret code. "He said 'peacemaker'!" they whisper. We stick to words they are most likely to come across in Scripture, such as *kind*, *thoughtful*, and *truthful*. Get creative and use what works best for you.

Repetition is annoying to adults, but children thrive on it. They actually enjoy it. Repetition is soothing to their brains, because their brains are growing at such a fast pace. Constant new information makes them feel overwhelmed and frustrated.

I find myself saying "Make a wise choice" so many times a day that it gives me a headache. But I've taken the time to develop what it means, so that every time I say it the sweet meaning takes deeper and deeper root in their hearts.

Once you've explained a new word bundle to your kids, it's time to practice. If we're sitting at the table and I say "Be a gentleman" to one of my kids, I watch carefully to see what happens. If he continues to be impolite, I say, "Uh-oh. I think you forgot what a gentleman is. Tell me what a gentleman is. Do you think a gentleman would do what you are doing? How does being a gentleman glorify God?" I give *him* a chance to explain back to me everything we've already learned about our word bundle. Five minutes later I can say "Be a gentleman," and that's all it takes. He remembers exactly what it means.

My five boys are very physical. I like to take my word bundles and physically put them into their hands. I hold my hand closed, look my four-year-old in the eye, and say, "I'm going to give you your special job for the day. Are you ready?" His eyes sparkle and he says, "Yeah!" He holds out his hand, and I say, "Your job is: be quick to listen." I open my hand into his and close his hand around the imaginary word bundle. He giggles and holds his fist closed. I ask him what's in his hand, and he repeats it back to me. We take a minute to talk about what that phrase means. Throughout the day, as I work on that specific skill with him, I ask him what's in his hand and he remembers. Everything that "Be quick to listen" means comes back to him every time he hears that phrase, because I made it memorable for him.

Word bundles help you to take your discipline with you when you are not at home. At a restaurant, I can say "Be a gentleman," and I can expect to see an instant change in behavior. When my child runs up to me to tattle at a playdate, I say "Be a peacemaker," and he runs off to play, armed with all the tools of peacemaking.

Word bundling will make your life so much easier, but that is not ultimately the point. Word bundling creates hooks in your kids' brains. Right now "peacemaker" is a hook. On it we hang everything we want to teach our kids about peacemaking: thinking of others first, sharing, and not tattling. As they grow, we can add more information to the hook, layering on what's already there. Right now they are practicing peacemaking with their brothers. One day it will be with coworkers, bosses, and eventually their wives. Give your kids the hooks now. Start with simple definitions and build as they grow.

Reflection

1. Think of a specific character trait or habit you want to work on with your child. What story, from either the Bible or another source, can you use in order to help teach this trait?

2. What are some word bundles that you already use or would like to start using? Write out the phrase you will purposely use over and over and everything you want to teach your kids about what it means.

Word Bundle	What It Means

10

Sibling Fights: Can My Kids Really Be Best Friends?

I was thrilled when I found out my second baby was going to be a boy. We already had one boy, and I started dreaming of the beautiful friendship they would share. I couldn't wait for him to be old enough to play with his brother. They were only fifteen months apart, so I knew I wouldn't have to wait long. I remember the first time I heard them making each other laugh. Seeing the special smiles they put on each others' faces made my heart sing. I could see a lifelong brotherly bond forming. But with the bonding came something I was totally unprepared for: the fighting.

And I mean *fighting*. There were days when all I would do was break up fights. Their screams were my alarm clock. My husband and I thought we were going to have to raise our children in separate rooms just to keep peace in the house.

I wasn't just frustrated; I was heartbroken. I didn't want to separate my children. I wanted them to enjoy being together, just as we enjoyed being with them. But that natural foolishness they were born with was running rampant in their interactions with each other. We couldn't keep separating them, and we couldn't keep refereeing. It was time to give them some tools.

Peacemakers and Peacebreakers

The sibling fighting reached a climax by the time I had three boys, ages four and under, and another one on the way. I was desperate. One morning I gathered them on my bed with some art supplies. On a big piece of a cardboard box, I drew two categories: Make Peace and Break Peace. I drew a happy heart on one side and a broken heart on the other. I told the boys that peace means joy. It means quiet. It means sharing love. "The best kind of peace in the whole world comes from Jesus. When we trust in him, he takes away our sin and gives us special peace. Since we have peace from Jesus, we want to have peace with our brothers, too." I drew some silly stick figure pictures of the boys and spread them out on the bed. "I want you to tell me if the boys in each picture are making peace or breaking peace."

One by one they helped me decide which side of the chart to glue the pictures to. I picked situations that were very applicable to them: grabbing toys, knocking down someone's tower, pushing, throwing food, and so on. They got it. I was shocked. They spent the rest of the day running back and forth to the chart to see whether what they were doing was making peace or breaking peace. They would identify their actions in the picture and tell me which side it was on.

We have continued to develop this idea as they've gotten older. Making peace isn't always about getting justice. It's not about protecting your rights. Sometimes people are unfair. Sometimes they make you angry. How can you take that situation and make peace? That silly chart (which has been ripped apart and glued back together numerous times) has taught my boys that peace doesn't mean getting your way. It often means making a sacrifice in order to stop the fight. When one of the boys comes running up to me, wailing about what a brother did, the first thing I ask is "What did you do to make peace?" Usually they stare at me sheepishly. I tell them to go back, make peace the best they can, and then come back to me if it doesn't work. They rarely come back.

A huge temptation for me is to hyperfocus on *what* they are fighting about. Who had the toy first? Who had a turn last time? Who broke the rules of the game? It's helpful to have this information, but I have to remind myself that all of it is beside the point. The point is, how are they showing love to one another?

Yesterday one of the boys broke the rules of Candy Land. The other brother freaked out and declared war. Once we sorted through the details and everyone calmed down, both brothers had to own up to their part of the broken peace. It wasn't just about "who started it." Both brothers had to think about how they were making each other feel.

Put Words in Their Mouths

"No! Stop it! That's *mine*. Give it to me!" Without some guidance, these are the only things that little ones would say to each other. They don't know what else to say. Their words are fueled by their selfishness. We have to teach them. We have to give them the words and show them how to use them.

In our family, we started by outlawing the above words. We tell our boys there are always other options. We taught them three peacemaking phrases that they can use in any disagreement:

- "Can I please have a turn?"
- "You can have a turn when I'm done."
- "Please stop."

These words have become so rote in our house that even the two-year-old says them. If they resort to peacebreaking words, we tell them to try again. Every angry word must be replaced with a gentle word. It takes practice. *Lots* of practice.

The older kids have graduated into the subtler nuances of their words. Recently I've been able to teach them the differences between positive and negative words. All negative words, such as *no, not, don't, can't, won't*, and *doesn't*, can be replaced by positive words. At breakfast this morning, a little brother said, "I'm eating Cheerios." The big brother was quick to correct him. "No, you're not—" I stopped him mid-sentence and reminded him to use positive words. He thought about it and said, "Yes, your cereal does taste like Cheerios . . . even though it's actually Rice Krispies."

I was with another mom recently, and I heard her tell her daughter, "That is not a respectful way to talk to Mommy. What should you say instead?" I was so encouraged by this mom's response. She knew that her daughter needed to be taught, and she was giving her a chance to practice. Tell your kids how to speak when they are angry or hurt. Teach them how to ask for what they want. It will impact every relationship they have—both now and when they are adults.

Team Mentality

Last year our kids started getting more involved in group activities. We had to have the inevitable "bully" talk. Since our boys are so close in age, they will go through life doing a lot of the same activities together. We started teaching them that one of their special jobs as brothers is to defend one another against bullies. "You have to watch out for one another. If you see some-one picking on your brother, go help your brother out." This les-son serves a dual purpose. Not only do they feel confident around bullies, but they learn not to be bullies in their own home. "Hey, you're supposed to protect your brother, remember?" When they hurt each other, they remember they are acting like a bully—the very thing they are supposed to protect each other against.

I've seen the team mentality go both ways in families. The goal is family unity, not family pride. When families take it too far, it leads to kids thinking their family is better than anyone else's—that their decisions are better and their rules are better. "A Wallace child should never act that way!" is a good example of what we don't want to do. It's not about us. We're a team not so that we can serve ourselves better, but so that we can serve the body of Christ better. We get to teach our kids to be part of God's family (the church) by starting with our own family. Ulti-mately this looks like service.

- Don't walk away from a brother who is hurt.
- If you're playing with a toy that your brother wants, help him to find another toy.
- If you're getting yourself a drink, ask your brother if he wants one.
- If you finish your chore before your brother does, help him to finish his.

When we notice the kids doing these things, we say "Good work, team!" The Christian life is not individualistic. Teaching a team mentality within the home prepares kids to participate in the visible expression of the gospel here on earth: Christ's body, the church.

A Better Way to Say Sorry

Have you ever met someone who can't apologize? Or maybe you are that person. Apologizing is difficult. We want our kids to practice this now so that it carries over into their relationships with their spouses, coworkers, bosses, and friends. What better way than to have them practice on their siblings?

In the Wallace house, there are plenty of opportunities to practice. Today I heard the four and the six-year-old fighting. I came into the room to see them glaring at each other. Not knowing what had happened, I said, "What do you need to say to each other?" The six-year-old sighed and said, "I'm sorry I squeezed your face." The four-year-old nodded and said, "I forgive you. I'm sorry I called you a scoundrel." Scoundrel? I didn't even know he knew that word. I had to stifle a laugh. Sure, there are worse things they could do and say to each other, but they were still trying to hurt each other however they knew how. Their relationship needed mending.

We want to get at the heart of the matter when our kids fight. It's not about who had the toy first. It's about how we affect others with our words and actions.

In our home, an apology is not complete until four things have happened.

1. Both parties make eye contact with each other.
2. The offending party says "I'm sorry for . . ." (Be specific.)
3. The offended party says "I forgive you."
4. Both parties hug.

This goes beyond a quick fix. It is a lesson in love and humility. Ultimately, you can't always solve your kids' fights. What you can do is give them the heart tools they need in order to solve their fights themselves. Instead of demanding who had the toy first, ask "Who is showing love in this situation?" Or "Are you blessing your brother or frustrating your brother?" Help your kids take a step back and see the spiritual side of their disagreement.

Now that my boys are a little older, I can legitimately say that they are best friends. Do they still fight? Every day. But they also look out for each other, seek to serve each other, and are armed with loads of peacemaking words and phrases that often stop the fight before it starts. Don't give up. It's a process, but it's worth it.

Reflection

1. Think of a recurring fight your kids have with each other. What is the heart issue? (Examples: selfishness, greed, trying to annoy, and so on.)
2. Write out three phrases that you want to teach your kids to replace the wrong words they are currently saying to each other.
3. Read Ephesians 4:2–3. Write out this passage in your own words, in a way that your children could understand, and share it with them.
4. How does teaching our kids about peace with Christ connect with their making peace with each other?

11

What to Do When Your Child Tells You No

I tend to complicate things for myself when it comes to discipline. I come at it backward. I compartmentalize sin into categories and try to come up with a discipline plan from there. "How should I handle lying? How should I handle hitting?" But, when I take a step back, I can see that my kids' sin falls into one basic category: rejecting my authority and God's authority in their hearts. This helps me to ask a different, more fundamental question: how should I respond when my child rejects my authority?

When I was growing up, there was one word that brought all the hustle and bustle of our household to a dead halt. It was when I or one of my siblings answered a parental instruction with the word *no*. Everyone stopped moving. Everyone stopped talking. A hush settled over the home as my parents turned to look at the child responsible. Sometimes my parents would quietly say, "What did you say?" As a parent now myself, I admire their subtle tactics. It was a way to convey how out of place that word was in our home. My siblings and I quickly learned that that response was not acceptable.

Why camp out on this word? Because if we take all our sin and boil it down, this word is at the heart of all disobedience to God. Dealing with this word should be a foundational part of our discipline plan. Before we can lay the groundwork for dealing with tantrums, rebellion, or disobedience, we have to do battle with this word. God made our children to be creative, thoughtful individuals with personalities and opinions all their own—and we want to hear them. But, as a response to a direct instruction given by a parent, *no* is not an option.

In Scripture, we see many examples of people who said no to God and the consequences that followed. Their lives were a mess. We can trace the mess of their disobedience back to when they told God no. Take a look at the directions God gave and at the people who disobeyed:

> God: Do not eat from the tree of knowledge of good and evil.
> Eve: No (Gen. 2:17; 3:6).
>
> God: Speak to the rock, and water will come out.
> Moses: No (Num. 20:8–11).
>
> God: Go to Nineveh and preach forgiveness of sin.
> Jonah: No (Jonah 1:1–3).

These examples make the Bible sound like a book about toddlers! But these were men and women who chose to say no to God. Because they were God's children, we can read on and see how he graciously redeemed their disobedience for his own glory. But they missed out on blessing and caused pain for themselves and their families. We also see many examples of people who said yes to God.

God: Take your family and move to a new place you have
never been.
Abraham: Yes (Gen. 12:1–4).

God: You will give birth to my Son.
Mary: Yes (Luke 1:35, 38).

God: Preach in places where people are trying to kill you.
Paul: Yes (Acts 23:11).

Oh, how my heart longs to answer like these people did. Sometimes our *yes* is bold and excited. Sometimes our *yes* is pure faith mixed with pain, like when Jesus said, "Not my will, but yours, be done" (Luke 22:42). This is where our children desperately need our instruction. They don't understand the concept of obeying out of faith and love. They will naturally say no every time they don't feel like obeying. It's our job to train their thinking now so that, as adults, they are ready to say yes to God.

The Power of *No*

The word *no* is powerful. It is often the first word kids learn, because they can sense that power. Our toddlers love to run around the house saying "No no no no no no no" just for fun. It's adorable. But there is a time that our children are not allowed to use that word, and it is when Mommy and Daddy give a direct instruction.

- "Go put on your shoes."
- "Come to Mommy."
- "Please go wash up for dinner."

If your child says no to the examples above, it might be tempting to think, *Well, maybe she just doesn't feel like it right now.* That's not the point. The point is that our kids need to learn to trust and obey no matter what. One day your kids might tell you no when it will cost them something more than being late for dinner.

- "Don't cross the street yet; there is a car coming."
- "Point the scissors down when you carry them."
- "Don't touch Mommy's curling iron."

Little ones don't know the difference between the two sets of examples given above. They have no idea which situations are dangerous and which ones aren't. They only know whether they have to obey or not. "You don't say no to Mommy and Daddy" is a frequent statement used around here, followed by discipline.

When we teach our kids not to tell us no, the point is not that they aren't allowed to tell us how they feel. It's our responsibility to teach them that there are appropriate ways to express their negative feelings. We teach them how to politely ask for other options. We show them how a respectful tone sounds. But, most importantly, we teach them to trust our authority.

Think about that word—*authority.* As parents, we are the ones holding all the authority. But we must remember that we are *under* authority as well. The authority that we have has been entrusted to us by another. We didn't earn it, and we certainly don't deserve it. Because our authority reflects God's authority, we are accountable to him for how we use it—and he takes it very seriously. We see an example of this in Matthew 18. In this parable, a master forgives his servant a great debt. The servant then goes out and abuses his fellow servants in order to make them pay back what they owe him. The words from the master are a sobering reminder to all of us: "You wicked servant!

I forgave you all that debt because you pleaded with me. And should not you have had mercy on your fellow servant, as I had mercy on you?" (Matt. 18:32–33).

As we exercise authority over our children, we do so as servants. We have a master who is watching how we treat those under us. We must see our authority as a gift to our children—something that helps and blesses them. This will remind us never to use our authority in a prideful, self-serving way.

Teaching Independence without Losing Respect

You might hear the word *no* most often when you try to help a toddler do *anything.* Toddlers have a strong desire to be independent, and they are ready to lash out if they feel like their independence is being threatened. This drive to be independent is not a bad thing. It's actually a gift from God. I didn't appreciate it when I had my first baby; every time he wanted to do things on his own, I would sigh and think, *I can do this for you so much faster! We're in a hurry!* But, because my son was driven to be independent, he learned how to do things for himself very quickly.

I have since had a child who was the opposite: he let me do everything for him. While it was nice not fighting the battle, I soon realized I was setting myself up for a different battle later on. By the time I had another baby, this son should have been more independent, but he wasn't. It was difficult to inspire him to be a "big boy." Independence is something to be nurtured and encouraged. How can we foster that spirit of independence while instilling in our kids submission to our authority at the same time?

It all comes down to their attitude. If your kids are old enough to try doing things for themselves, they are old enough to learn how to ask in a respectful tone. My two-year-old is not very verbal yet. When I try to help him with his shoes, his first reaction is to scream and yank them out of my hands. He cannot form full sentences yet, so I taught him how to just say "Please?" It's a work in progress, because a child's natural reaction to frustration (especially when he doesn't know how to talk yet) is anger. He's not actually angry with me for helping him put his shoes on; he's angry because he so desperately wants to try on his own but feels helpless and out of control. When he grabs the shoe and screams, I gently take the shoe back and say, "Would you like to put your own shoe on?"

"Yes!" he screams in frustration.

"You may put on your own shoe, but you need to ask Mommy respectfully. You say, 'Mommy, can I please do it myself?' Try it. Say 'Please?'"

Now his frown dissolves into a smile, and he says, "Please?"

"Very good! Yes, you may put your own shoe on. You are such a big boy."

This is a way I can show my son that his independent spirit is special while still showing him that Mommy is in charge. The temptation as a mom is to discipline our kids for the angry reaction without taking time to equip them with appropriate responses. We don't do them any favors if we tell them what they did wrong without telling them how to do it right.

Independence is a team effort, and we are on the same team with our children. We share the same goal: more independence for them. It sometimes feels like we are on opposing teams, because they want *all* of their independence and they want it *now*. They want to soar like a kite in the wind. But we keep the string of the kite very short when they are little. As they grow, we let it out a little more and a little more. We let them explore and gain independence under our instruction and shepherding.

To the world this sounds suffocating and stifling. It sounds like we are hampering our kids' independence. But we know that if we let our little ones reject our authority now, they will reject it when they are older. If we let our little ones say no to our authority, what hope do we have of them obeying us when they are older? That is like letting all the kite string out too soon and then struggling to pull it back in. It creates bitterness and frustration, both for us and for our children.

Communication

My oldest son was my most verbal toddler. He quickly learned that talking was the best way to communicate how he felt. It was fascinating to hear him put his baby emotions into words: "Mommy, I love you, but I'm angry, and all I want to do is hit you in the face." When he told me that at barely two years old, I couldn't believe it. But rather than fly off the handle, I said, "Thank you for telling me how you feel. It's good that you didn't hit Mommy in the face, even though you wanted to. That is good self-control. I'm proud of you."

If our kids make an effort to use their words, we should be quick to encourage them. We aren't teaching them to never be angry or disappointed. We're teaching them how to handle their feelings in an appropriate way.

When the baby screams "No!" and throws his food on the ground, I say "No, no. You don't say no to Mommy, and you don't throw your food. Say 'All done, Mommy!'" Then, as he looks at me with a blank expression, I wipe his face and send him off to play. I don't force him to say it then and there, especially if it is a brand new concept. I model it for him for the first several times. The next time he throws his food, I repeat the same instruction, this time with discipline. Pretty soon he starts to think twice about throwing his food. He might think twice and do it anyway, but the foundation is being laid—one brick at a time.

Our children are not robots. We want to hear from them. We want to know their likes and dislikes. Through the beautiful process of getting to know them, we also have to show them that they are under a loving authority: us. In the little years, obedience training lays the foundation for that trust.

As we teach our kids to communicate, we do not just tell them when *not* to say no. We also need to teach them a very important time *to* say it. They are learning that this word has weight. As they learn not to say no within the loving parent-child relationship, they might naturally begin to think that this is the way they must behave with everyone. It's our job to teach them that that's not true. "No" is a way for children to protect themselves. We tell our kids to say no to strangers who ask them to come with them, or if someone wants to touch them in a way that makes them uncomfortable. It's a tricky balance to teach our kids when to say no to other adults, but we can't leave that part out. We teach them that they can trust us that but that they don't have to trust everyone. This gradually helps them learn the difference between saying no to other adults for self-protection and saying it out of rebellion against Mom and Dad.

Sassy, Strong-Willed Toddlers

No can take many creative forms with our kids. It can be anything from a shake of the head to a "Whatever, Mom." But the standard remains the same: Don't say no to Mom and Dad. Is this a battle worth fighting? Yes. Is it a hill to die on? Yes. Our authority points to God's authority. God's authority is the only foundation we have to build our discipline on. But a battle doesn't always have to be bloody. My friend Carlee shared with me an awesome example of how she conveyed her authority to her daughter in a fun, creative way. Here's Carlee's story:

One of the benefits of my husband's first job as a youth pastor was taking our first child with us to everything. Church was without a doubt her second home and the students were her very best friends. But the drawback was that she sometimes heard words or ideas that we would have preferred she didn't. Add in a strong will, and we were often in for it.

One day after youth group when she was about two I told her to go get her shoes on. Instead of saying, "Yes Mommy," or more often, "No!" she said, "Whatever." Hands on the hips, head tossed to one side—the whole deal. My first instinct was to tell that sassy girl never to say that again. But if you have a strong-willed toddler, you know that the word "Never" is equivalent to "Always." Instead, I told her this:

"What a fun word! 'Whatever' is so fun to say! But sometimes when we say 'whatever' it's funny, and sometimes it is disrespectful. So, when Mommy or Daddy tell you to do something, you need to say, "Yes." But, when we are being silly, you can say, 'Whatever.' Let's practice: Oh my goodness! There is a purple elephant on the deck!"

{She ran to see}. "No there's not!" she told me.

"I know! That's when you say, 'Whatever!' Let's try again: A pink striped panda bear just ran by!'"

"Whatever, Mom!"

"Right!"

"The dog has pink ears!"

"Whatever!" {Now we are giggling}.

"Okay, go get your shoes on . . ."

I wish I could tell you she said, "Yes, Mommy," and did it. Instead, of course, she wanted to play the "whatever" game. It took several tries and some correction to get those shoes on willingly. However, she did not tell us "whatever" with inappropriate sass again.

It's okay to feed the imagination and playfulness of children. Yes, it led to a few moments when her lack of discernment caused her to say "whatever" at the wrong time. But in general, she got to use this fun new word, and we had a fun new game, that ended up helping us teach her some good decision making. At the dinner table we would say a few funny things, and then a serious one. She practiced how to reply to each one.[1]

Carlee didn't back down from her standards—her daughter was not allowed to talk to her in a disrespectful way. But Carlee was able to use a fun way to show her daughter the importance of obeying authority.

Reflection

1. Why is independence an important part of godly character?
2. Choose a scenario in which you give a direct instruction and your child tells you no. Reflect on your game plan.

Scenario ("Put on your shoes"; "It's time for us to go home"; etc.):

   a. How will you communicate to your child that the response was not appropriate?
   b. What will you teach your child to say instead of no in this specific scenario?
   c. What is an appropriate consequence in this situation?

12

Tiny Ones and Tantrums

My first experience handling tantrums happened when I was fourteen. I was babysitting three little kids. It had been a long day, and we all wanted to get out of the house. Their mom had left me with some money and said they could pick out a treat from the store. We took a short walk over to the store around the corner. *This will be great,* I thought. *They each get to pick whatever they want. They are going to love this.* Little did I know just how wrong I would be.

We got to the store and went to the candy aisle. Each child immediately grabbed a candy. I was expecting excitement, but the looks on their faces weren't happy. It was more like they were panicked. They quickly put the candies back and picked different ones. Then they picked different ones again. Then they didn't just want to pick *different* ones; they wanted *more.* As we finally made our way to the checkout, they were clutching greedily at their candy and bickering with each other. By the time we paid and left, two were still fighting and one was cry-ing—all while still holding handfuls of candy. I was completely bewildered. "They have candy. Why are they all throwing fits? What more do they want?"

But I already had the answer. *More.* More is exactly what they wanted. More options, more control, more everything. These kids were not used to boundaries and authority in their home. All options were open to them all the time.

Children don't know what to do with that much freedom. It makes them miserable. It brings out their greed, selfishness, and discontentment. Remember those bumper strips that keep the bowling ball from rolling into the gutter? A little one with too much freedom and not enough authority is a bowling ball heading straight for the gutter. A tantrum is a sign of a child saying, "I am miserable—not because I can't have the toy I want but because I don't feel secure. I don't know who's in charge. I don't know where my boundaries are. I'm going to push all the way to the edge to see if there is anything there to keep me safe." That's our cue as moms. That's our chance to show them that, yes, they are safe. Yes, there are boundaries. No, tantrums will not be tolerated in this home. And your child's sweet heart breathes a sigh of relief.

When I hear the word *tantrum*, I immediately think of kicking, screaming, and howling. A child can have a meltdown like this for many different reasons, as we will see. But, for the purpose of our discussion, we are going to focus on the rebellious side of tantrums. It's not ultimately about the kicking and screaming. It's about a heart that willfully pushes away authority.

Ignoring Tantrums

It's common advice to ignore a tantrum in order to show your child that he or she won't get more attention for it. But there are several reasons why it's a problem to ignore a tantrum and why we choose not to do so in our home.

Ignoring Tantrums Creates a Power Struggle

The tantrum becomes all about who can stand their ground the longest. The toddler is writhing on the floor screaming, and Mom has her back turned, doing the dishes. Who will give in first? In a Christian home, the authority has already been established. It's not about who has more endurance. Mom is in charge, not the toddler.

Ignoring Tantrums Ignores the Heart

Our ultimate goal in parenting is not about showing our kids the best way to get what they want. That only addresses the actions on the surface. "If you ask nicely, you can have the toy. If you throw a fit, Mommy will walk away and ignore you." It's not about how to get the toy. It's about pointing our kids to God. God does not ignore sin. When the child throws a tantrum, we need to communicate this message: "What you are doing is wrong. You are not in charge. Mom is in charge of you, and God is in charge of all of us. You obey God by obeying Mom."

Ignoring Tantrums Disrupts Peace in the Home

While Mom and toddler are engaged in this power struggle, what are the other family members doing? Everyone is exposed to the screaming. It is damaging to the home. The toddler knows it. "Mom won't listen to me, but I'm still going to wreak as much havoc as I can." Can a little one really think this way? Oh yes. When you ignore the tantrum, you give your child the power to continue to be destructive.

Addressing Tantrums: ACT

Tantrums should be addressed. But how? While tantrums might be messy and exhausting, they are far from hopeless. With five little boys in the house, I have experienced a wide range of tantrums. There are three tools that help me tailor my response to each child's individual personality and needs. When a tantrum hits, I use ACT: Alone time, Cause, Teach.

Alone Time

Alone time is not just different from ignoring a tantrum; it is an essential first step to dealing with the heart. When a tantrum first erupts, take your child by the hand and lead him to a quiet place to be alone. Say, "Your response is not appropriate. You sit in here alone until I come and talk to you." Emotions are high—for both you and your child. Discipline in the heat of the moment is not very effective. Instead, give your child some alone time. This is an intentional *first* step to dealing with a tantrum. A spanking or other consequence might very soon follow. But that initial moment of alone time serves several important purposes.

It says that tantrums are not okay. Alone time communicates, even to the very young, that their behavior is not appropriate. Being suddenly alone is significant for a little one. For some personalities, that might be discipline enough. They don't want to miss the fun. They don't want to be away from their friends. When my almost-two-year-old throws a fit, I put him in his crib and close the door. When I come back five minutes later, he is holding his arms up to me, usually still crying. I say, "Are you ready to have a happy heart?" He knows that means he is about to get picked up, so he smiles and says, "Yes!" Before picking him up I say, "When Mommy tells you it's time to pick up toys, you don't fuss at Mommy. You say, 'Yes, Mom.' Can you say that?" He smiles even bigger and says, "Yes, Mom!" Then I know it's time for him to come out. All of a sudden, picking up toys feels like a giant privilege to him, compared to being alone in his crib. I take him back to the spot where he first threw the fit, and I give him the same direction. This time, he chooses to obey.

It gives your child a chance to calm down. You might decide that a spanking is the right consequence for the situation, but a spanking is not very effective if your child is already screaming and crying. The goal of the spanking is to show your kids that, because you love them, you cannot accept what they are doing. If you spank in the middle of a tantrum, there is a good chance that this message isn't sinking in. Let your child calm down so that emotions don't cloud their thinking. Take time to communicate your message before and after the spanking.

It gives you *a chance to calm down.* You need a moment away from the chaos so you can make a wise decision. I've noticed that between the first moment my kids throw a fit and five minutes later, my discipline strategy changes significantly. That's because my initial reaction is based on *their* initial reaction. I'm driven by emotion. I need a minute to be away from them so I can be objective and intentional about my discipline. My goal is to shepherd the heart, not just to make them stop screaming. Alone time also gives me a chance to determine the next step: Cause.

Cause: Why Is My Child Throwing a Fit?

Tantrums are always fueled by something. Although a tantrum is never an okay response, its cause should help to determine the discipline. Why is your child throwing a fit? What sparked it? What's going on under the surface?

A few days ago, son number three started screaming at the lunch table. I sent him out of the room, annoyed that he was disrupting lunch. I assumed he was overreacting to someone bugging him, like he usually does. When I went to talk to him, I asked him what was wrong. "I bit my tongue!" he sobbed. I wrapped my arms around him and held him close. I was kicking myself for immediately getting annoyed with him. I was also so glad that I took the time to talk to him before launching into discipline. I rocked him and told him I was sorry his tongue hurt. In this situation I wouldn't classify his reaction as a tantrum—but it can be hard for us moms to tell the difference in the heat of the moment. Always look for the cause. (In children who have experienced emotional trauma, however, it can be much more difficult to determine the cause of tantrums. These children might require a different approach altogether.)[1]

My kids are the most emotionally fragile when they are tired or hungry. That doesn't excuse their tantrums, but it reminds me that sometimes meeting physical needs comes before addressing spiritual needs. I had never fully experienced the "terrible twos" until child number four hit them—and he started six months early. While I was taking steps to teach him appropriate responses other than tantrums, I also dug around for clues as to why he was upset. Yes, he is a sinner, and he does not like to be told what to do—but there was more to it than that. I realized that he was going through a major growth spurt and was hungry *all* day long. Every time his blood sugar got low, he fell apart. I can relate. I started giving him healthy snacks between meals, and he had a complete turnaround. He knows that I am willing and able to meet his needs, which makes him feel less helpless and frustrated. That doesn't mean that every time he threw a fit I handed him food without any further instruction. Meeting his physical need always went hand in hand with giving him instruction and discipline.

This gets tricky. As parents, we juggle managing hearts and

bodies at the same time. We can't let tantrums slide just because our kids don't feel well, but we also can't demand a perfect attitude from them without actively seeking to meet their physical needs. (And, in some cases, physical needs go beyond eating and sleeping. If your child has regular meltdowns and can't communicate with you about what's wrong, check with your pediatrician to see if there could be underlying physical issues.)

Tantrums can become a habit overnight. If a tantrum gets your child exactly what he wants when he wants it, then he will use tantrums for everything. So what do you do? That's when we move on the *T*: Teach appropriate responses.

Teach Appropriate Responses

The final step, Teach, also means discipline. Once you have instigated Alone time and determined the Cause, it's time to decide what form of Teaching (or discipline) your child needs. When my son bit his tongue, he screamed in pain, not rebellion. The difference is crucial when you are deciding how to discipline. He needed a hug, not discipline. But what about when my kids scream in rebellion?

Example: You tell your child it is time to put toys away. He throws his body on the floor and kicks and screams and says "No! No! No!"

Time to ACT.

A. Take your child by the hand and say, "That is not an appropriate response. Go wait on your bed until I come to talk to you."

C. You look at the clock. Yep. It's already a few minutes past bedtime. He's exhausted, and that's contributing to the tantrum. That doesn't excuse his rebellious attitude, but it helps you make an informed decision about discipline. You decide, *He still needs to obey, but he can't mentally process cleaning up an entire room right now. How can I stick to my original direction, for him to put his toys away, but simplify it so that it's something he can be successful with right now?* You go to your child, make eye contact, and say calmly, "I know you are tired, but you may not tell Mommy no. I want you to clean up three toys and then get back in your bed. Do you understand?"

T. Time to teach. What discipline would be appropriate? At this point you might decide to spank your child for telling you no. If you think your child is too emotional and tired for a spanking to be effective, you might decide sleep is the quickest way to resolve this discipline situation. Then, over the next few days, you can keep a close eye out for similar situations. Is this becoming a habit, or was it purely related to his being tired? Be ready to step up the discipline if you notice that it's becoming a habit.

Sometimes a natural loss of privileges might seem like the best course. Our kids know that if they fuss at the food we set in front of them, it will be taken away (temporarily) and they will have to sit at the table with no food. The situation, the personality of your child, and how well he already knows better will help to determine the fitting consequence.

Reflection

1. Read Job 5:17. What is the connection between blessing and correction? How are tantrums a symptom of our children despising our discipline?
2. Think of a time when your child is the most prone to throwing a tantrum. Write out your strategies for ACT.

Situation (park, friend's house, bedtime, etc.):

A—Alone time (Where? How long? How would you explain it to your child?)

C—Cause (What usually prompts the tantrum in this situation?)

T—Teach (What discipline do you think is appropriate? What would you say to your child in order to address the heart here?)

13

Big Kids and Rebellion

I recently saw a YouTube video of a teenage boy throwing a tantrum. He was raging against his parents for taking away his video games. He threw a full-blown fit that reminded me of my toddler—except it was much bigger and scarier.

I wish that tantrums had an age limit, but they really don't. Kids don't naturally grow out of them. Tantrums simply take on a new form. It's the adult yelling and honking on the freeway. It's the outraged customer screaming profanity into the phone at customer service. How we handle tantrums now can have a huge impact on how our kids act as teens and adults. But what do we do when our big kids throw fits? If we continue addressing tantrums head-on and don't give up, we can help our kids avoid becoming teenagers and young adults who still throw fits against authority.

As kids get older, their bar of accountability naturally rises higher. We can expect more from them, because they understand more. But this isn't the time to take a back seat and say, "You should know better. I've already taught you what to do." This is the time to dig in and take our discipline to a deeper level. When our kids are little, they learn that "because I said so" is reason enough to obey. As they get older, we get to develop their understanding of authority. Now we can say, "I want to tell you where my authority comes from and why it's important to you."

Covenant Love

"Because I said so" is reason enough for us to obey God, isn't it? And yet God, in his fatherly love, lets us in on his plan for obedience. He shows us in his Word *what* obedience does for us and *why* we should obey. That doesn't mean that obedience is open for negotiation. It means that we obey most happily within the bounds of a deep and loving relationship. How can we communicate that to our older kids?

You won't find the word *tantrum* in the back of your Bible, but we definitely see examples of tantrums in Scripture. God's people threw major fits in the desert when they got tired of the manna (see Num. 11:4–6). Moses whacked a huge rock with his staff when he got angry (Num. 20:10–11). What did God do with this rebellious people? God, in his holiness and mercy, drew his people into a covenant with himself. He said, "Obey my voice, and I will be your God, and you shall be my people. And walk in all the way that I command you, that it may be well with you" (Jer. 7:23).

Now this is where things get exciting. As parents, we get to mimic that same beautiful covenant love with our children. Listen to the similarities between Exodus 20:12 and the covenant we just saw between God and the Israelites: "Honor your father and your mother, that your days may be long in the land that the Lord your God is giving you." I love the addition that Ephesians 6:2 adds to this commandment: "This is the first commandment with a promise."

What is the common promise we see for both the Israelites

who obeyed God and children who obey their parents? It's the promise that it will be well with them. This is the glorious truth we get to share with our older kids. When our big kids rebel with tantrums, we explain covenantal love. "When you act out in rebellion against my authority, I cannot keep you safe. When you obey me and accept my authority, things will go well for you."

Our six-year-old had grown past the tantrum stage—or so we thought. It recently popped up again out of the blue. He was adjusting to having yet another baby brother in the house messing with his stuff. He was genuinely frustrated and was looking for an outlet for his frustration. While accepting that his feelings were real and that this was a difficult transition, we had to let him know that tantrums were not an option. Important groundwork had to be laid.

The perfect opportunity came one day when one of his little brothers destroyed his beloved Tinkertoy sword. The six-year-old fell apart. He screamed and thrashed around the room, overcome with anger and frustration. My first reaction was to jump straight to the *T* (teach) and dole out a consequence. He should know better, right? Thankfully, my husband was home and he whisked my son out of the room. My son was given his much needed *A* (alone time), while my husband talked patiently through the *C* (causes) with him.

When I went up a few minutes later to see what the verdict was, I found my husband and my six-year-old sitting on the bed talking and giggling. Daddy was recounting to our son a time when his own younger brother had smashed his Lego pirate ship—on purpose. My son, who was blinded by rage just moments before, was cracking up.

"So," said Daddy, "sometimes that's what little brothers do. I know it makes you mad, but there are other things you can do instead of screaming. Can you think of an example?"

"Hmmm," our son thought. "I could ask him nicely to please stop?"

"That's a great idea," said Daddy. "Sometimes that will work, and sometimes it won't because your brothers are so little, but I want you to always talk gently to them. You may not scream at them. Mom and I will help you find special places to keep the things you build so that they won't get wrecked as often. If you scream at your brothers instead of talking kindly and asking for help, you will lose the privilege of playing with your Legos."

"Okay!" he said as he hopped off the bed and ran to salvage the rest of his Tinkertoy creation. If we give our big kids a solid plan to fall back on, they are less likely to throw a tantrum.

Time to Listen

As parents, we usually stick to the same script when our toddlers throw fits: "That's not how you ask. That's not how you answer. That's not the way you say it." We are constantly teaching them to use their words instead of their fussing. We tell them over and over that there is a better way to communicate. So, as they grow and mature, we need to show them that it's worth it. It has to pay off for them. They need to see that respectful communication is better than tantrums. How can we show them that? By listening.

Yesterday I told my five-year-old to close up the iPad and get ready for outside time. I saw his shoulders slump. He obeyed, and then he quietly came to me and said, "Mom, can I please have a few more minutes to play my game on the iPad?" This was a huge breakthrough. His go-to response is usually to fuss and whine, resulting in restricted iPad time. I could tell that he was making a conscious decision to be respectful and self-controlled. I said, "I love the way you asked. That was very respectful. Yes, I would love to give you a few more minutes." His face brightened, and he ran back to the iPad.

In this situation, I wanted my son to connect submission to authority with immediate blessing in a very tangible way. There are other times when my kids make a huge effort to use their words instead of throwing a fit, and I say, "I love the way you asked! But no, you may not do something different. I love you, and I am very proud of you!" It's important for them to know that I will listen to them, even if it doesn't change the plan.

Isn't that the graceful way that God deals with us? He bends his ear to hear our desires (see Ps. 116:2). He *listens*. We don't deserve his attentive, loving ears, and yet we have access to them all day and all night.

One way to motivate big kids to trade tantrums for words is to teach them how to name their feelings. When I sense the rumblings and I know the volcano is about to blow, I say, "Are you feeling angry right now?" Sometimes just the acknowledgment of their feelings is enough to calm them down. If they insist on throwing a fit anyway, I say, "I can't help you until you can tell me what's wrong. Go to your room and think about what words you would like to use." The more vocabulary we arm our kids with, the more they feel equipped to deal with their feelings using words instead of tantrums. I talk to my big kids about what it means to feel disappointed, frustrated, and vengeful. Whether the feelings are justified or not is beside the point. They need to know how to identify their feelings so they can talk things out and ask for help.

This doesn't mean kids should be allowed to say whatever they want just because they are angry. They still need to speak respectfully. As our big kids learn to trade tantrums for talking, it's a great opportunity to teach them the power of *good* words. A helpful verse to discuss with them is Ephesians 4:29:

"Let no corrupting talk come out of your mouths, but only such as is good for building up, as fits the occasion, that it may give grace to those who hear." This helps them learn how to talk about their feelings as a way to seek help rather than as a way to vent.

One of my sons has held on to the tantrum stage longer than the others have. His go-to response for any kind of frustration is to throw his head back and howl. The older he gets, the more ridiculous it seems. But as his vocabulary grows, he's able to identify what he needs and ask for help before he reaches his limit. Last week he came up to me and said, "Mom, can I take my toys into another room and have some alone time?" He sensed his frustration bubbling up (due to too many brothers hovering around), and he was able to head it off at the pass. This was a huge improvement. I made an effort to protect his alone time and keep his brothers away from him for a little while. I wanted to show him that he can come to me for help.

Help your older kids know that you are always willing to listen to them. Help them to see that throwing a fit is a waste of their parents' attentive ears. Go overboard to give them your full attention when they make an effort to speak about their frustrations. They need to see that it makes a difference. I want my kids to know that if they choose to speak calmly, they will be met with attentive listening.

Reflection

1. Read Leviticus 26:3–12. List the blessings connected with obedience.
2. Using that list for inspiration, jot down some ideas to share with your big kids about how their obedience can bring blessing to their lives.

3. Read Psalm 116:1–2. What characteristics of our heavenly Father can we imitate from this passage when our children communicate their distress to us?

4. If you have kids who have continued to throw tantrums past the toddler stage, reflect on what practical tools they might need, whether it's more vocabulary words, more alone time to think, or more one-on-one time to talk.

14

Three Ways to Practice Follow-Through

Every mom has struggled with consistency in discipline. I came into the living room the other day and saw my sweet four-year-old stretched out on the couch. He was so calm, so quiet. He was peacefully staring off into space. I sighed and thought, *Wow. I love it when he's like this—just taking time to be still and think and slow down a little.* He looked at me and smiled. I smiled back. Then he said, "Mommy, can I get out of time-out now?"

"Oh," I gasped. How long had he been there? I couldn't even remember *why* he was there. "Yes, honey. Now go play nicely this time." Fail.

Consistency is the dam that keeps all our discipline from running downstream away from us. When I feel like my discipline isn't working and I get the urge to try a fresh approach, I remind myself, "Consistency over creativity." My kids don't need more creative rules and consequences. They just need me to be consistent with the ones I've already made.

Consistency depends on us. Another term for consistency is *follow-through*. Once you've created a wonderful discipline system, how do you ensure that it actually happens? Giving your kids a new rule is like teaching them to play catch. You wouldn't toss the ball and then turn away. You would wait to see whether they catch it. That's follow-through. But life gets busy, and sometimes you feel like you are throwing balls all day and don't have time to see where they land. In the beginning, some groundwork might need to be laid, but follow-through can quickly become second nature.

Before

Prep work is a crucial part of our follow-through. Before we can practice follow-through, we have to have a plan to actually follow through *with*. Our expectations need to be clear, both to ourselves and to our kids. What do we expect of our kids in this situation? What do we want to teach them, and what are the tools we need in order to help us do it?

Think about everything you do to get the kids ready to head out the door. Shoes: check. Clean diaper: check. Potty: check. Jackets: check. Faces wiped: check. Hearts: . . .

It's easy to leave the most important prep work undone. Before we leave to go to the store, a birthday party, or church, we do a little heart prep. We remind our kids what kind of behavior we expect from them at this particular event. We remind them what the consequences will be for disobeying. This is important, because if your child is used to a specific time-out seat at home, they might think you will leave discipline at home with the time-out seat. Tell them when, where, and how they will be disciplined away from home. They need to know that discipline comes with you.

We don't want this to be a burdensome lecture for our kids. If you are in the beginning stages of this or have never done it before, then yes, it will require some lecturing. You have to take time to lay the groundwork. Now that our kids are used to these reminders before we go anywhere, we can keep them short and positive. We like to let them participate in the discussion and keep it fun.

Parents: Where are we going right now, kids?

Kids: Kiera's birthday!

Parents: What is the first thing you say to Kiera when we get there?

Kids: "Happy birthday!"

Parents: What are some of the fun things we are going to do there?

Kids: Cake, presents, and the bounce house!

Parents: Right. There are going to be a lot of fun things. There are also going to be a lot of kids. Do we run around and scream and grab the other kids?

Kids: No!

Parents: If someone bumps you in the bounce house, do you push them back?

Kids: No. We say, "Excuse me."

Parents: When it is present time, do you touch the presents?

Kids: No!

Parents: When Mom and Dad tell you it's time to go home, what do you say?

Kids: We say, "Okay!"

Parents: What happens if you do not have self-control at the party?

Kids: We have a time-out and we miss the fun.

Parents: That's right. So let's go have some fun!

When I don't remember to do this with my kids, I notice a huge difference. All of a sudden I look around the party at my wild bunch of boys and think, *What happened to my children?* Then I remember we've forgotten to get their hearts ready. Oftentimes we pull into our destination and take a few minutes in the car to do our heart prep.

Morning is often the best time for moms to practice this *before* step. For moms who work or moms who send their kids to school, this is your window to equip them with valuable tools. As you pack their lunch boxes, think of a few simple truths to pack in their hearts. Perhaps this is when you mention a few scenarios that might come up during the day and let your children talk about how they would handle them. What Scripture passages could they tuck in their hearts to help them handle those scenarios? What struggles or worries could you pray with them about before they step out the door? We'll see in a moment how taking time for *before* will pave the way for a beautiful *after* discussion at the end of the day.

During

If possible, we should be ready to hold our children accountable *during* an activity. I was at a birthday party recently with all my kids. I was talking with my friends, and my kids were playing happily with their friends—or so I thought. Another mom walked up to me and said quietly, "I'm sorry to interrupt, but your son won't let my daughter in the playhouse. I only mention it because she's been asking him over and over, and he keeps telling her girls aren't allowed." I looked over, and sure enough, there was my five-year-old, king of the playhouse, deciding who could and couldn't come in.

This mom's tone was so gentle and nonjudgmental. I felt like we were on the same team. I was thankful that she brought to my attention a specific skill I've been working on with my son: kindness. He gets caught up in the game and starts to treat people like his action figures. Sometimes he doesn't like it when his friends have thoughts of their own.

While I was glad that she brought this to my attention so I could address it, I wished I had caught it myself. It's impossible for us to catch everything, especially in a busy social setting. That's why we need each other as moms on the same team.

Here is a test I use for myself to see if I am following through with discipline *during* a social activity: Are other parents catching more things about my own kids than I am? Do I often overhear another parent asking my child to please not hit? Do I glean most of my information about my child's behavior from other parents' comments or other kids' tattling? If I am the one responsible for their discipline and training, I have to be aware of what my kids are doing.

The opposite extreme would be a "helicopter mom." This is the mom who never leaves her child's side in a social setting. Perhaps she's afraid of what her child will do or what another child will do to him. The problem the helicopter mom creates is that there is no opportunity for her child to actually practice. We have to let the leash out enough for our kids to practice what they're learning. Our kids are going to fail. I wasn't happy with the fact that my son was slamming the playhouse door in his friend's face, but I was thankful for the opportunity to work with him on a real-life example. The point is not to control our kids like robots so they never fail, but to be ready to address their failures in a timely way.

I try to strike the balance between being oblivious to what my kids are doing and being a helicopter mom during my daily structure with the kids. While they are moving through each phase of our daily structure, I'm putting dishes away, folding laundry, changing diapers, and searching Pinterest for recipes to help me use up leftovers. But my ears are always perked up. The eyes in the back of my head are working overtime. I don't just listen to the words my kids are saying to each other; I listen for tones and attitudes. When I know they are off playing, I try to always be aware of *what* they are playing. All day long I read between the lines of what I see and hear to determine how their hearts are developing.

Yesterday I sent the kids to their rooms to read books quietly while I made a phone call. The phone call went longer than I expected. It suddenly occurred to me that the muffled screams and thuds coming from the bedrooms didn't sound like reading. But I was distracted, and I allowed it to continue until the end of my phone call. Sure enough, when I went to check on the boys, they were having a wrestling match. They had books in their hands, but they were using them as weapons. As I thought back to when the sounds started, it had been only about five minutes into the phone call. That's when I should have excused myself for a minute to practice follow-through with my kids.

My lack of follow-through undid some groundwork. My kids learned that I can say one thing, but that when I'm distracted it doesn't carry any weight. In this situation I disciplined my kids for not obeying, and I worked in some extra quiet reading times this week so we can practice and relearn. I don't do my kids any favors when I don't follow through. We all suffer the consequences.

Now, life is going to happen. Sometimes there will be things that take a higher priority than immediate follow-through. One time I was having a conversation with a friend, and she was sharing with me about how she was struggling with her faith. I was aware that my children were behaving less than ideally in the background, but I needed to give all my attention to my friend at that time. Yes, I would have to work harder with my kids later, but I might not have that opportunity with that friend again. God will give us wisdom about how to prioritize our follow-through. Sometimes it will be immediate; sometimes it might have to wait. But we need to make it happen, one way or the other.

If you're not already practicing follow-through, it might take some time to train your eyes and ears. Take a few days to set everything else aside and be that helicopter mom until you become more naturally aware of what's going on in your kids' hearts. If you identify with the helicopter mom, take a step back and allow your kids to succeed and fail on their own. It will give you much more insight into what's really going on in their hearts. Then you can step in to address their hearts more specifically.

After

How can we use successful follow-up *after* an activity? In our home, it usually takes the form of questions and discussion.

- "How did you decide to use your free time?"
- "Were you kind to your brother outside? What did you do that was kind?"
- "How did you show thoughtfulness to your friend when he came over?"

If you've been away from your kids all day, use your *before* to guide your follow-up questions. Did your children encounter any of the scenarios that you talked about at breakfast? Were they able to use the Scripture that you talked about? How about what you prayed about together? What specific ways did they see God giving them strength or wisdom today?

These follow-up questions can give us important insight into what's going on when we're not around. Before I was an Awana leader in the same room as my son, I used to ask him if he obeyed in Cubbies. He always said, "Yep!" He wasn't trying to deceive me, but he wasn't quite old enough to reflect on his actions. He just knew what I wanted to hear. I started asking, "What did your teacher say to you in Cubbies today?" He said, "She told me to stop talking." That was my "Aha" moment. We needed to work on listening and not talking. But I wouldn't have known that if I hadn't used follow-up questions. I used this as a springboard to teach my son how to reflect on his own actions. Now my kids are so used to me asking them how things went that they're already asking themselves that question before they even get home. I can tell that I've gotten out of the habit of intentionally following up with them when I have conversations like the one I recently had with my four-year-old.

> Four-year-old: I'm very sorry, and I will never do it again.
> Me: Do you remember what you did?
> Four-year-old: Nope.

It's up to me to teach my kids how to reflect on their actions until it becomes a habit for them.

This final step is also important if your child is learning something new. In our home the transition from naps to quiet time is a big deal. Each time my kids have outgrown their naps, my follow-through has been a crucial part of a peaceful transition. My two-year-old just took the plunge. He knew that quiet time was a big-boy privilege, and he was excited. We did our *before* by talking about what quiet time should look like. We did our *during* by correcting behaviors that weren't appropriate for quiet time. Then we did our *after* by discussing how it went.

"Did you use your quiet time wisely? What was your favorite part? What do you think you could do better next time?"

When we involve our kids in this step, it inspires them to take responsibility for their actions. My two-year-old loves talking to me about his quiet time. We emphasize the parts he does well so that he sees reflection as a positive thing. He is learning how to reflect on his behavior in a productive way so that he can either change something that is wrong or continue doing what is right. If we teach our kids how to learn from their successes and their failures when they are young, it will become part of their character as adults.

Reflection

Choose a phase in your daily structure (breakfast, quiet time, bedtime routine, and so on), an outing, or a special activity in which you want to practice more consistent discipline. Write out your strategy for follow-through.

Activity:

Before:

During:

After:

From One Mom to Another:
As You Keep Going . . .

I wish I could grab a cup of coffee with you and laugh and cry over how crazy and difficult it is to raise up these precious children in the fear and admonition of the Lord. We could swap stories, sigh, and shake our heads in awe at the mystery of grace. I love knowing that moms like you are taking this journey with me.

I am regularly overwhelmed by discipline with my crazy crew. Just when I think I've got a handle on things, my kids throw something new at me. But when my feet start to shift on the sands of my emotions and misplaced expectations, the gospel brings me back to solid ground. One look at Christ diffuses my frustration and reminds me what it's all about. Discipline is ultimately about my kids' relationship to God, not to me. I have this brief opportunity to use discipline in order to teach them all about sin, grace, and the character of God.

This helps me to remember that discipline isn't a one-time, quick fix. I'm in it for the long haul. True heart change comes from many, many layers of consistent and faithful building on the truth. That fact gives me a lot of peace on days when I discipline all day long and can't see any visible results. It reminds me that my work in the Lord is not in vain (see 1 Cor. 15:58). He has a plan for my discipline. He is working through it—on days when I can see it and on days when I can't.

A dear friend of mine, who now has grandchildren and great grandchildren of her own, became a Christian when she was in her twenties. She told me her mom used to sit with her during her rebellious teenage years and talk to her about the gospel. Over and over again her mom would come alongside her and share truth and a listening ear. My friend said, "At the time, I wasn't listening. I really didn't care about what she was saying because I didn't believe in it. But it left a huge impression on me that she was there for me. She never gave up." When she became a Christian years later, everything that her mother said finally clicked. It was always there, buried deep down—the seeds of faith planted by her mother.

You, dear faithful mama, are a seed planter. Your task is not easy, but it is very simple: keep planting. On your own, your heart would be crushed under the weight of this responsibility. But you are not on your own. In Christ you have been blessed "with every spiritual blessing in the heavenly places" to do what God has called you to do (Eph. 1:3). You don't have to reinvent the wheel or blaze new trails. You can simply walk in the path of faithfulness that God has already laid out for you, trusting the results to him.

My hope is that the word *discipline* has lost some of its gloom and mystery—that it has become less burdensome and yet more compelling. As you move forward, remember what your discipline truly is: a beacon pointing your children to eternal life. In every discipline situation, look for ways to point your kids back to Jesus—to his perfect righteousness and his forgiveness.

There is one final thought I want to leave you with—from one mom to another. It is this: don't underestimate the power of a mother's prayers. When we've done all that we can for our children, prayer is the only thing we can still *do*.

D. L. Moody once said, "The impression that a praying mother leaves upon her children is life-long. Perhaps when you are dead and gone your prayer will be answered."[1]

The more I come to grips with how little control I have over my kids' lives, the more I fall in love with prayer. There is a Father who *is* in control of every aspect of my kids' lives, physically and spiritually, and he is willing to listen to me. He can sort the trivial from the eternal. He knows what's actually best for my kids and for his glory.

We don't know God's plan for our kids, but we do know that he has chosen to work through our prayers. James 5:16 says, "The prayer of a righteous person has great power as it is working." Don't know where to start? Take a look at the verses in the appendix in the back of this book. I keep a printout of them in my Bible so that I can give it to other moms. If there is a weapon that is always sharp, always ready for the spiritual battle, this is it.

So as you shepherd, discipline, and guide, don't forget to pray, pray, pray. We have the ear of the King. Let's use it for our children.

Appendix

How to Pray for Your Children

If we think of our discipline as seeds, then prayer is the water. All day long I plant seeds, and at night when my kids are in bed I water the seeds with prayer. Just as seeds can't grow without water, successful discipline is impossible without prayer. But when I sit down to pray for my kids, my biggest question is: where do I begin? There are so many things that I want (and don't want) for my kids. But I've noticed that if I launch straight into my wish list, my prayers can actually produce more anxiety than peace. I start micromanaging God in my prayers by praying for all the what-ifs I can think of. Before I know it, I'm a mess of anxiety, thinking of all the horrible things that could happen and how to prevent them. I forget about the ultimate goal: to make my child like Jesus. When I take a step back and focus on this goal, it helps me pray for what I don't know in the context of what I *do* know. Like this:

1. I don't know that my child will never experience a heartbreaking loss. I do know that God "heals the brokenhearted and binds up their wounds" (Ps. 147:3).
2. I don't know that my child will get a good job and be

153

financially stable all his life. I do know that God "is a shield to all who take refuge in him" (Psalm18:30 NASB).

3. I don't know that my child will avoid every devastating disease. I do know that "those who wait for the LORD will gain new strength; they will mount up with wings like eagles" (Isa. 40:31 NASB).

This helps me to leave the hypotheticals behind and pray God's faithfulness over my kids. My prayers become less about what could happen and more about who God is. I can pray God's discipline over my kids, knowing that his discipline is fueled by the greatest love of all.

My favorite tool that helps me pray for my kids is the prayers that Paul prayed for the churches. Paul always knew what to pray for his spiritual "children." Read these rich words and insert your kids' names. Bathe them in prayer and in Scripture. Build up walls of strength and protection for them while they are still too young to even know that they need it. While so much is out of your control, this is something you actually *can* do for them—something that God has promised will have eternal results.

> May the God who gives endurance and encouragement give you the same attitude of mind toward each other that Christ Jesus had, so that with one mind and one voice you may glorify the God and Father of our Lord Jesus Christ. (Rom. 15:5–6 NIV)

> May the God of hope fill you with all joy and peace in believing, so that by the power of the Holy Spirit you may abound in hope. (Rom. 15:13)

> But we pray to God that you may not do wrong—not that we may appear to have met the test, but that you may do what is

right, though we may seem to have failed. For we cannot do anything against the truth, but only for the truth. For we are glad when we are weak and you are strong. Your restoration is what we pray for. (2 Cor. 13:7–9)

I do not cease to give thanks for you, remembering you in my prayers, that the God of our Lord Jesus Christ, the Father of glory, may give you the Spirit of wisdom and of revelation in the knowledge of him, having the eyes of your hearts enlightened, that you may know what is the hope to which he has called you, what are the riches of his glorious inheritance in the saints, and what is the immeasurable greatness of his power toward us who believe, according to the working of his great might. (Eph. 1:16–19)

For this reason I bow my knees before the Father . . . that according to the riches of his glory he may grant you to be strengthened with power through his Spirit in your inner being, so that Christ may dwell in your hearts through faith—that you, being rooted and grounded in love, may have strength to comprehend with all the saints what is the breadth and length and height and depth, and to know the love of Christ that surpasses knowledge, that you may be filled with all the fullness of God. (Eph. 3:14, 16–19)

And it is my prayer that your love may abound more and more, with knowledge and all discernment, so that you may approve what is excellent, and so be pure and blameless for the day of Christ, filled with the fruit of righteousness that comes through Jesus Christ, to the glory and praise of God. (Phil. 1:9–11)

And so, from the day we heard, we have not ceased to pray for you, asking that you may be filled with the knowledge of his will in all spiritual wisdom and understanding, so as to walk in a manner worthy of the Lord, fully pleasing to him: bearing fruit in every good work and increasing in the knowledge of God; being strengthened with all power, according to his glorious might, for all endurance and patience with joy. (Col. 1:9–11)

Now may the God of peace himself sanctify you completely, and may your whole spirit and soul and body be kept blameless at the coming of our Lord Jesus Christ. (1 Thess. 5:23)

To this end also we pray for you always, that our God will count you worthy of your calling, and fulfill every desire for goodness and the work of faith with power, so that the name of our Lord Jesus will be glorified in you, and you in Him, according to the grace of our God and the Lord Jesus Christ. (2 Thess. 1:11–12 NASB)

Now may our Lord Jesus Christ Himself and God our Father, who has loved us and given us eternal comfort and good hope by grace, comfort and strengthen your hearts in every good work and word. (2 Thess. 2:16–17 NASB)

Notes

Chapter One: The Game Plan: Let's Get Ready

1. James Strong, *Strong's Exhaustive Concordance of the Bible*, updated ed. (Peabody, MA: Hendrickson, 2009), Strong's number 3809.
2. See Lori Grisham, "'I'm Going to Stay Right Here': Lives Lost in Mount St. Helens Eruption," *USA Today*, May 17, 2015, https://www.usatoday.com/story/news/nation-now/2015/05/17/mount-st-helens-people-stayed/27311467/.
3. Tedd Tripp, *Shepherding a Child's Heart* (Wapwallopen, PA: Shepherd Press, 1995), xviii.
4. Michael Horton, *Ordinary: Sustainable Faith in a Radical, Restless World* (Grand Rapids: Zondervan, 2014), 18.
5. Elyse M. Fitzpatrick and Jessica Thompson, *Give Them Grace: Dazzling Your Kids with the Love of Jesus* (Wheaton, IL: Crossway, 2011), 54.

Chapter Two: Why We Don't "Punish" Our Kids

1. See Jessica Miller, "Utah Boy, 16, Fighting 1-to-15-Year Prison Sentence," *The Salt Lake Tribune*, May 26, 2014, http://archive.sltrib.com/article.php?id=57972054&itype=CMSID.
2. Paul Tautges, *Brass Heavens: Reasons for Unanswered Prayer* (Adelphi, MD: Cruciform Press, 2013), 33.
3. Tedd Tripp, *Shepherding a Child's Heart* (Wapwallopen, PA: Shepherd Press, 1995), xviii.

4. Arthur W. Pink, *Comfort for Christians* (repr., Lafayette, IN: Sovereign Grace, 2007), 38.
5. Doug Thompson, "When God Uses Pain to Train" (sermon, Middletown Bible Church, Middletown, CA, June 2012), available online at https://player.vimeo.com/video/43907489.

Chapter Three: Rewards and the Gospel

1. John Piper, "How Much of My Sinful Past Should I Tell My Children?," Desiring God, May 26, 2015, http://www.desiringgod.org/interviews/how-much-of-my-sinful-past-should-i-tell-my-children.
2. Susan Hunt, *My ABC Bible Verses: Hiding God's Word in Little Hearts* (Wheaton, IL: Crossway, 1998), under the "L" entry.
3. Andrew A. Bonar, *Memoir and Remains of the Rev. Robert Murray M'Cheyne* (Edinburgh, 1894) 293.

Chapter Four: The Right Kind of Fear

1. C. S. Lewis, *The Lion, the Witch, and the Wardrobe* (1950; repr., New York: Macmillan, 1970), 75–76.
2. Timothy Keller, "What Does It Mean to 'Fear' God?" (Q&A session, Redeemer Presbyterian Church, New York City), available online at http://download.redeemer.com/rpcsermons/QandA/What_does_it_mean_to_fear_God.mp3.
3. Jen Wilkin, "Women, Trade Self-Worth for Awe and Wonder," Desiring God, July 14, 2016, http://www.desiringgod.org/articles/women-trade-self-worth-for-awe-and-wonder.
4. Rachel Watson, "Utter Dark Sayings to Your Children," The Gospel Coalition, November 30, 2015, https://www.thegospelcoalition.org/article/utter-dark-sayings-to-your-children.

Chapter Six: From Emotion-Led to Spirit-Led Discipline

1. John Piper, "Is It Possible to Be Angry and Not Sin?," Desiring God, July 8, 2009, http://www.desiringgod.org/interviews/is-it-possible-to-be-angry-and-not-sin.

Chapter Seven: Setting Our Expectations

1. Paul and Karen Tautges, *Help! My Toddler Rules the House* (Wapwallopen, Pennsylvania: Shepherd Press, 2010), 11–12.
2. G. I. Williamson, *Catechism for Young Children: An Introduction to the Shorter Catechism* (Horsham, PA: Great Commission Publications, 1991), 4.

Chapter Eleven: What to Do When Your Child Tells You No

1. Carlee is a pastor's wife and a mother of three. For more of her thoughts on parenting, visit her website: http://www.carleerussell.com/.

Chapter Twelve: Tiny Ones and Tantrums

1. When it comes to helping children with trauma, my trusted friends who have adopted recommend the following Christian resources: Karyn B. Purvis, David R. Cross, and Wendy Lyons Sunshine, *The Connected Child: Bring Hope and Healing to Your Adoptive Family* (New York: McGraw-Hill, 2007), which comes with a highly recommended study guide and helpful DVDs; Diane Langberg, *Suffering and the Heart of God: How Trauma Destroys and Christ Restores* (Greensboro, NC: New Growth, 2015); and Linda J. Rice, *Parenting the Difficult Child: A Biblical Perspective on Reactive Attachment Disorder* (O'Fallon, IL: SeedSown Press, 2014).

From One Mom to Another: As You Keep Going . . .

1. D. L. Moody, *Glad Tidings: Comprising Sermons and Prayer-Meeting Talks* (New York, 1876), 355.